GLOU(... & CHELT_NHAM TRAMROAD

and the
LECKHAMPTON QUARRY LINES

THE
GLOUCESTER &
CHELTENHAM
TRAMROAD

and the
LECKHAMPTON QUARRY LINES

by

David Bick, BSc, MIMechE, FSA

THE OAKWOOD PRESS

First Edition Published 1969
Second Enlarged Edition 1987

Printed by S & S Press, Abingdon, Oxford.

IN MEMORY OF

MY FATHER,

EDWIN EWART BICK.

Published by
The OAKWOOD PRESS
P.O.Box 122, Headington, Oxford.

Contents

Preface

"Of ancient writ unlocks the learned store
Consults the dead and lives past ages o'er"
Pope

Nearly two hundred years ago an enterprising landowner laid down tramroads at his quarries on Leckhampton Hill near Cheltenham. The innovation provided a stimulus for a much more important development, the Gloucester & Cheltenham Tramroad, which was one of the first public railways in England for conveying coal and goods pulled by horses. As a boy I heard old men talk of it, although beyond the memory of them all.

The line had been at work for nearly 30 years when steam railways came to Gloucestershire in 1840, but well before that time experiments with the new mode of locomotion were conducted over its metals. Though the track was taken up as early as 1861 its influence

A fine impression by Michael Blackmore of the *Royal William* passing through Windmill Hill Cutting during its trials. (*See Chapter 6*)

both economically and by simple physical presence was profound, and as the towns expanded ribbon-like along its course miles of streets and roads became the tramroad's indelible memorial.

From so enterprising and important an undertaking might be expected a legacy of documentary evidence, but such is not the case. There was none of the new railway's glamour to attract the artist or reporter, and very few records worthy of the name survive. Indeed, at times it seemed as if there had been a positive conspiracy to wipe the old line altogether off the map.

To assemble a history from random scraps and countless minor sources has been a difficult task, which by its very nature can never be completed, only abandoned, by the futility of further search. Yet the more the work progressed the more certain appeared the conclusion that much of great interest was lost and irrecoverable. What would we not give for the diaries of that shadowy and illusive figure Benjamin Newmarch, with a finger in every pie, or the engine driver of the *Royal William*?

Nevertheless sufficient has come to light to give, it is hoped, a tolerably correct picture.

An author's first book holds a special place in his memory, and I am indebted to my publishers for the opportunity of revising and much enlarging the original edition of 1968. A new chapter discusses the ill-fated and entirely forgotten Cheltenham & Cotswold Hills Railway of 1811, which would have doubled the length of the tramroad, and upon which work may actually have commenced.

With a growing awareness of the amenity potential of Gloucester Docks, where the line began, this new edition is timely. I hope it will awaken interest in a line which once held its place among "the principal rail-ways in England and Wales."

Though the concern was officially the Gloucester & Cheltenham Railway Company, the line itself was nearly always referred to as a tramroad, and this distinction will generally be observed throughout.

DAVID BICK, 1986

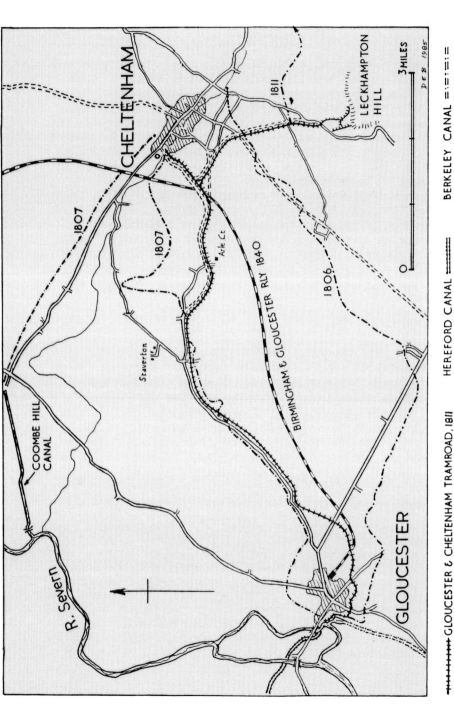

CHELTENHAM

LECKHAMPTON
HILL

1811

1807

1807

Arle Ct

BIRMINGHAM & GLOUCESTER RLY 1840

1806

Staverton

COOMBE HILL
CANAL

R. Severn

GLOUCESTER

D E B 1985

3 MILES

GLOUCESTER & CHELTENHAM TRAMROAD, 1811   HEREFORD CANAL   BERKELEY CANAL

PROPOSED TRAMROADS   TRYE'S TRAMROAD   NEW ROADS

Transport developments to 1840, including tramroads proposed but not built.
The Cheltenham and Cotswold Hills line is on the extreme right.

Chapter One
Prelude to the Tramroads

Britain has for long possessed so extensive a network of roads and railways that it is difficult nowadays to conceive the enormous problems involved in conveying heavy goods and merchandise in earlier times.

Not until early 18th century did the better roads of the turnpike trusts begin to supplant the rutted and uncertain tracks. But these new roads were no real answer to the growing freight traffic, whose ponderous nature frequently rendered them almost impassable. A solution eventually came in two forms, the canal and the horse railway, both of which utilised the draught animal's efforts to much greater effect and, at the same time, relieved the roads of their most damaging traffic.

These two forms were largely complementary. Horse railways often belonged to canal companies and acted as feeders and distributors for the waterborne cargoes. After 1800, however, many new lines were financed and controlled independently of the canals, one being the Gloucester & Cheltenham Tramroad, and the events leading to its construction will now be related.

Two hundred years ago, Cheltenham was a small market town of some 2,000 inhabitants. Of no particular merit, it began to attract visitors after a certain Mr Mason discovered mineral waters which were claimed to be beneficial to health. He sold the waters and his son-in-law, Captain Skillicorne, built the first Pump Room. The town's reputation as a watering place began to spread, its fame being assured by the visit of George III in 1788.

The constant flow of visitors encouraged new building, and streets and squares of elegant Regency dwellings with numerous humbler properties, discreetly distant, were soon being laid out. This activity created a great rise in demand for raw and bulk materials, especially stone and coal. Although the nearby Cotswold hills provided first class stone for building it was not hard enough to withstand traffic on heavily used roads. For such purposes carboniferous limestone from the Avon Gorge near Bristol was much preferred and was shipped up the Severn to the quay at Gloucester. Forest of Dean coal was also brought by river to the quay, and Staffordshire coal, another source of Cheltenham's fuel, came downstream to Tewkesbury. Whether landed at Gloucester or Tewkesbury, these commodities finally had to be carted at great expense eight or nine miles to the town, and the cost of carriage almost precluded the use of coal on the Cotswold hills beyond.

7

As elsewhere, the roads were practically impassable in winter and eventually became so ruinous that His Majesty's Mail Coach was directed to take another route, avoiding Cheltenham completely. But before this lamentable situation arose, remedies were already being discussed and resulted in an Act of Parliament, obtained in 1793, for a canal from the Severn near Wainlodes, directed towards the town.

A glance at the map suggests that the River Chelt would have provided the obvious course but this was not adopted, perhaps due to opposition of the mill owners. Instead, the promoters merely applied for powers to build a canal two and a half miles long to the foot of Coombe Hill, through which a considerable cutting was required for access from the basin to the turnpike road to Cheltenham.

The canal, suitable for barges up to 70 tons, opened about 1796. It was never more than a qualified success and other attempts were soon made to fulfil its purpose. In 1801 a canal was proposed from Tewkesbury to Cheltenham, an idea which several times recurred, but failed for want of support.

But, by this time, interest was turning to the other means of transporting heavy loads. Charles Brandon Trye, the owner of Leckhampton Hill, was supplying the growing Spa with building stone and, to help his quarries along, had laid tramroads and an inclined plane near the hilltop. These tramroads were probably the inspiration which led to the following announcement in the *Gloucester Journal* of 25 August 1806.

> Notice is hereby given, that a meeting of the Subscribers of the intended Railway from Cheltenham to Gloucester, will be held on Tuesday, 26th inst., at the Plough Inn, Cheltenham.

The route, surveyed by Hall & Son, ran east from the dock basin of the unfinished Gloucester and Berkeley Canal, and crossed Ermine Street near Brockworth. It then took a more northerly bearing past Shurdington Church to a spot near Sandford Mill, to the east of Cheltenham.

Proposals were made to apply for Parliamentary powers to authorize the line, but Sir William Hicks, a local landowner, encouraged strong opposition. Nevertheless, by March, 1807, the project was being favourably received in many circles including the Corporations of both Gloucester and Cheltenham. The Gloucester and Berkeley Canal Co., then twenty years from completing its undertaking, realized that the tramroad could only be beneficial to trade, and gave its blessing.

Perhaps with the view to placating Sir William, the first route was now completely revised by a different surveyor, Daniel Trinder. It

ANNO QUADRAGESIMO NONO

GEORGII III. REGIS.

* *

Cap. 23.

An Act for making and maintaining a Railway or
Tramroad from the River *Severn*, at the Quay in
the City of *Gloucester*, to or near to a certain
Gate in or near the Town of *Cheltenham* in the
County of *Gloucester*, called *The Knapp Toll Gate*,
with a Collateral Branch to the Top of *Leckhampton Hill* in the Parish of *Leckhampton* in
the said County.   [28th *April* 1809.]

WHEREAS the Town of *Cheltenham* in the County of *Gloucester*
is become a Place of great public Resort, and the Number of
Houses and Buildings in the said Town and Neighbourhood
have of late Years greatly increased and are rapidly increasing : And
whereas the Turnpike Roads in the Neighbourhood of the said Town
have been greatly injured and destroyed by Carriages travelling thereon,
laden with Corn and Coals, and with Stone and other heavy Materials
for building, and the Turnpike Roads between the City of *Gloucester* and
the said Town of *Cheltenham*, owing to the constant Draught of such
heavy Materials thereon, are now in a very dilapidated and ruinous State,
and if a Railway or Tramroad was properly formed and made from the
River *Severn*, at the Quay in the City of *Gloucester*, through the several

[*Loc. & Per.*]   Town-

The title page of the Act authorising the Gloucester & Cheltenham Tramroad.

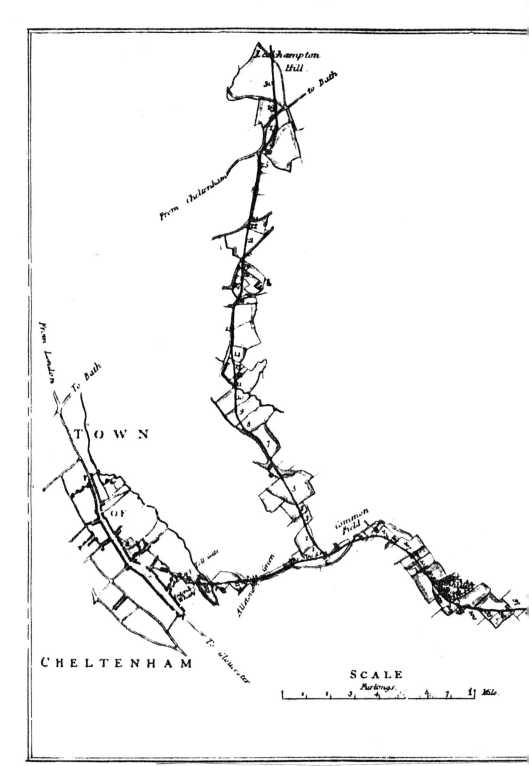

The route of the tramroad as finally adopted.

PLAN

of an intended

RAIL OR TRAM ROAD,

from

GLOUCESTER to CHELTENHAM

with its

COLLATERAL BRANCH.

Surveyed by D. TRINDER,

1808.

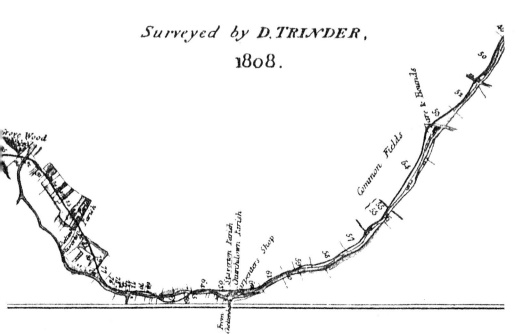

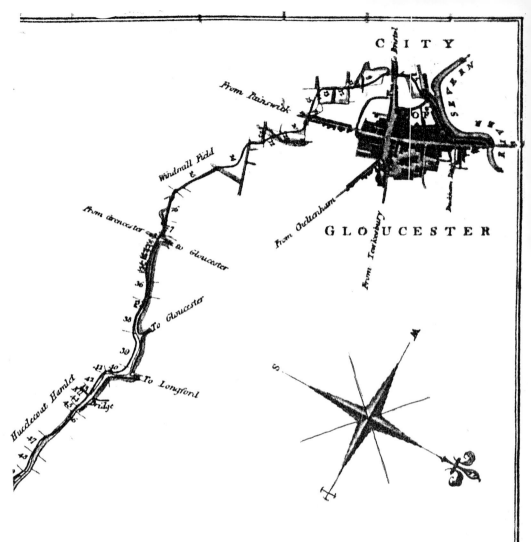

EXPLANATION.

The Red Line is the intended Rail or Tram Road.
The Length from the Bason of the Berkeley Canal, to the
intended Wharf at Cheltenham is 8 Miles, 6 Furlongs & 7 Chains.
Ditto including the whole of the Quay is 9 Miles & 4 Chains.
Ditto Collateral Branch is 2 Miles, 6 Furlongs.

Engraved by J. Basire.

circumvented Gloucester around the north and followed the turnpike road towards Cheltenham. In those days the road took its present course for several miles, as far as the Plough Inn where it crossed Staverton Bridge, and entered the town from the north-west via Hayden Hill. Trinder's line left the road at Staverton Bridge, pursued a winding but easily graded course through Fiddler's Green and terminated at the west end of the town.

Prior to the new survey, the Coombe Hill Canal owners, afraid that their trade would suffer, had conceived the idea of extending their waterway to Cheltenham, but the cost and the opposition of a land-owner led them to abandon the scheme.

They then decided, somewhat belatedly, to substitute a tramroad and eventually submitted a Bill to Parliament for the purpose. After the first half mile, the intended route ran through fields north of the turnpike road, to terminate in Swindon Road, Cheltenham.

Meanwhile the Gloucester–Cheltenham Tramroad protagonists were considering a deviation in their revised route "which (in the opinion of an experienced Engineer particularly conversant in Tram Roads) would prove of greater advantage to the Public, to the Land Owners, and to the different Roads in the vicinity thereof . . ."

The engineer was John Hodgkinson who later made the Hay Railway and other tramroads in South Wales. Acting on the opinion, Trinder considerably altered his route into the final form. Leaving the quay, it passed through the dock area at Gloucester, skirted the south of the city, and followed the turnpike road to Staverton Bridge. Beyond, a more direct route was taken across country to Cheltenham. A mile before its destination, a "collateral branch" left the main line to join Trye's lines on Leckhampton Hill, two and a half miles south of the town. Surprisingly, only in this last survey was the branch included.

According to Trinder's plan the length of the main line was eight and three quarter miles, or nine miles with the lines along the quay at Gloucester. The branch was two and three quarter miles.

Hodgkinson estimated the cost of the main line and branch at £25,261 14s. 0d. and the annual coal traffic at 22,000 tons. Time was to show that the price was badly understated but the tonnage only slightly so.

Whilst these revisions were under way, the Coombe Hill tramroad supporters took up the cudgels and a paper battle ensued, each side issuing lengthy pamphlets denigrating their opponents, with the facts suitably weighted where they did not happen to suit. But the Coombe Hill people failed to win enough support. The Bill was rejected in favour of the rival scheme which, in April, 1809, obtained the necessary Parliamentary powers to proceed. These powers, amongst the very earliest in Britain for the the construction of a public railway, were invested in

> An Act for making and maintaining a Railway or Tramroad from the River Severn at the Quay, in the City of Gloucester, to or near to a certain Gate in or near the Town of Cheltenham, in the County of Gloucester, called The Knapp Toll Gate, with a collateral Branch, to the Top of Leckhampton Hill, in the Parish of Leckhampton, in the said County.

The subscribers (shareholders) were as follows.

The Right Honourable James Lord Sherborne	10,000
The Right Honourable John Howard Earl of Suffolk and Berkshire	500
Sir William Hicks Baronet	500
Joseph Pitt Esquire	1,000
James Agg Esquire	500
William Nettleship Esquire	1,000
William Fendall Esquire	1,000
John Turner Esquire	1,000
Richard Collins Esquire	3,000
The Reverend Parkington George Tomkins LL.D.	500
William Capel Esquire	500
The Reverend Thomas Welles D.D.	200
The Reverend John Neale, Clerk	500
Mr Joseph Newmarch	1,000
Thomas Hullett Esquire	500
Thomas Gitton Esquire	500
Mr Thomas Smith	500
Richard Bowden Esquire	500
The Reverend Henry Wetherell	1,000
The Reverend Richard Wetherell	400
Thomas Gray Esquire	300
Peter Radley Jackson Esquire	200
Mr Edward Smith	200
Thomas Minster Esquire	400
Peter Ryder Minster Esquire	200
Mr John Villar	200
	£26,100

When the line was built it did not in fact end at the Knapp tollgate but a few hundred yards to the west, at the junction of what was later to become Market Street and Gloucester Road.

The company's seal depicted two men with pick, shovel and wheelbarrow, a boat, and a horse pulling four tram-wagons, the whole being an allegorical representation of the Leckhampton Quarries, the River Severn, and the Gloucester & Cheltenham Tramroad.

Above. The original watercolour painting of the design for the company's seal.
David Bick

Below. This impression from the seal makes an interesting comparison with the original. *GWR Museum, Swindon*

The focal point of the quarry tramroads from an old postcard, about 1908. Top Incline on right, line to No. 6 incline in foreground. (*See Chapter 7*)

A line of stone blocks, partially excavated, to Brownstone Quarry, with two tramplates placed in position.   *David Bick*

THE BOTTOM JENNY.

The foot of Bottom Incline about 1895. Here the Leckhampton branch met Trye's quarry lines. *The late A.T. Bendall*

Building the standard gauge line to the limekilns, 1922. Top Incline has been abandoned but Middle Incline remains in use. *The late T.F. Coke*

Priory Lawn, London Road, the home of Charles Newmarch which is now the Cheltenham Motor Club's headquarters. *David Bick*

The route of the Leckhampton Branch in Cheltenham, looking along Norwood Street, 1966. *David Bick*

Sherborne House near Northleach about 1820, the seat of Lord Sherborne. It is now converted into flats.

Though the seal has long since vanished, an impression survives in Swindon's Railway Museum. By a remarkable coincidence an original water-colour which must have formed the basis for the seal came into my hands some years ago, its significance hitherto not being appreciated. The painting bears the inscription *Gloucester and Cheltenham Railway Company*. Around the edge is written in pencil, *This to be engraved with Gloucester & Cheltenham to go round*. When we compare the two, its purpose can scarcely be doubted.

At the same Parliamentary Session, another Act was granted of immediate importance to Cheltenham. It authorised a new turnpike road from the town to meet the existing Gloucester road at Staverton Bridge thus avoiding the hilly and almost impassable route via Hayden. The chief purpose of course was to give better communication with Gloucester for passenger road vehicles including, no doubt, His Majesty's Mail Coach.

The turnpike road and tramroad Acts could well be termed parallel exercises. They were largely supported by the same people, and the new road was planned to run alongside the tramroad, taking advantage of its easy gradients and ready conveyance of stone for construction. Probably for the latter reason, work did not start upon it until the line was in operation.

A further point favoured the common route. Stone for the road's upkeep was to be carried toll free on the tramroad, by virtue of a clause in the tramroad Act.

The anticipated cost of the whole enterprise was £6,500, towards which Lord Sherborne and the tramroad company itself each provided £500. Apart from this financial interest, the company later became actively involved in three turnpike roads at Gloucester, undertaking in 1827 to look after and manage on behalf of the trustees the weighing machines on the Tewkesbury, Cheltenham and Cirencester roads, on the outskirts of the city.

Amongst the trustees of the new road were John Hodgkinson, its engineer, and the pioneer of vaccination, Dr Edward Jenner. The clerk to the trustees was Charles Newmarch, of whom more will shortly be told.

The benefits of the undertaking, great to the travelling public, did not manifest themselves to the promoters. Financially, the road never compared with its iron companion, and an Act was actually obtained in 1825 for a shorter route between Cheltenham and Gloucester — an improvement which did not come about till almost a century and a half later, by the building of the Golden Valley bypass.

Chapter Two

Lord Sherborne's Tramroad

Heading the subscribers to the tramroad company were the Right Hon. James, the first Lord Sherborne, and John Howard, Earl of Suffolk and Berkshire who had married Sherborne's daughter in 1803.

Lord Sherborne owned various estates in Britain and had his seat at Sherborne Park, near Northleach. He advanced £10,000 and later gained a controlling interest in the company. Other subscribers included William Fendall, a Gloucester banker and one of the committee of the Gloucester and Berkeley Canal company, Captain Thomas Gray, the Reverends Henry and Richard Wetherall, the converted Sir William Hicks and Mr Joseph Newmarch.

Although all these men, with the possible exception of Fendall, played a considerable part in the tramroad's history, the name of Newmarch deserves special mention. Joseph Newmarch and his four sons, Joseph, Charles, Benjamin and George, were for many years in the confidence of the Sherbornes and all except young Joseph became associated with the company.

Charles lived at Priory Cottage (now Priory Lawn) in London Road, Cheltenham. He acted as steward and solicitor to the Sherbornes and as clerk to the company until his death in 1823.

George took over his brother's duties of solicitor until 1839 and also acted for the company in 1836. He practised on his own account in the legal profession for many years in Cirencester and died in 1842. Benjamin Newmarch had a tumultuous career, interspersed with several financial crises. During more solvent periods, he leased the tolls of the tramroad and later became its agent or general manager. In 1820 he resided at Ragley Cottage in the Tewkesbury Road, not far from the tramroad depot, but by 1823 he had moved to No. 1 St George's Place.

The solicitors to the company comprised a partnership of three: Francis Welles, Theodore Gwinnett and Charles Newmarch, the latter having joined in 1806 or 1807, and on the initial committee of management were Sir William Hicks, the Wetheralls, Captain Gray and Benjamin Newmarch.

The tramroad company's first meeting was held in the Town Hall, Cheltenham, in May 1809; construction of the line started soon afterwards, and the ceremonious laying of the first stone block was conducted by the Earl of Suffolk and Berkshire on 21st November, 1809.

Initial efforts concentrated on the Leckhampton branch and that part of the main line from the junction to the terminal depot in

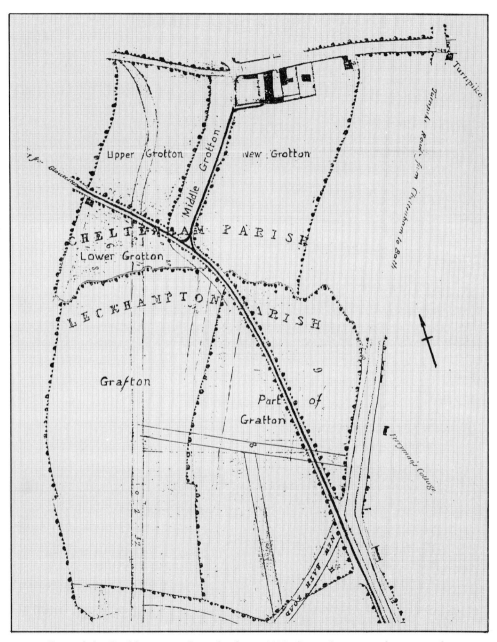

Part of the Leckhampton Branch about 1820. Several proposed new roads have been sketched in. Suffolk Road is at the top, Shurdington Road (New Bath Road) at the bottom. *GRO*

Cheltenham. The depot covered one and three quarter acres; the site is now bounded by Market Street and the Gloucester Road. Rapid progress was made and on 2nd July, 1810

> . . . the Tram Road, running from the platform near the summit of the Leckhampton-Hill to the town, was opened, and the first load of stone brought down . . . On arriving at the end of the Tram Road, the procession was met by a great concourse of persons, who hailed the welcome sight by loud huzzas — three times three; whilst a merry peal from the steeple announced the event to the neighbourhood . . .
>
> At Five o'clock about fifty gentlemen, of the first respectability, sat down to an elegant dinner at the Plough Hotel — the Honourable John Dutton, Son of Lord Sherborne, Lord of the Manor of Cheltenham in the chair.

We must now turn attention to the Gloucester end, where from the beginning the tramroad's destiny was intimately bound up with the docks, although according to Act of Parliament the line physically began at the riverside quay just beyond.

The dock formed the inland terminus of the Gloucester & Berkeley Ship Canal, upon which work had begun during the canal mania year of 1794. The directors included William Fendall and C.B. Trye. The latter had invented an excavating machine, but after a brief trial it was cast aside as "inadvisable". The company soon ran into interminable cash problems, and after finishing the dock and a few miles of canal southwards, work ceased for a number of years.

An early task for the Gloucester & Cheltenham Railway Co. was to reach the river as directly as possible, for supplies of stone blocks and tramplates from the Forest of Dean ironworks and quarries. To this end it shelved for the present the rambling parliamentary route to the quay, and instead gained authority for a route across a wooden bridge over the canal to Naight Wharf. Ground rent became due from Michaelmas 1809, suggesting that work on the line began then, even preceding the first ceremonial block-laying of November 1809. The short cut to the river is shown on Trophimus Fulljames' map of 1810.

Naight Wharf also flowered commercially, if only briefly. Apart from his interest in the tramroad, William Fendall had invested in the Bullo Pill line, opened in 1810 to convey Forest coal to the Severn below Newnham. To exploit the trade, Fendall and two other promoters of the Bullo Pill tramroad, James Jelf and Royston Jones, applied to rent the wharf. However, the Lydney & Lydbrook tramroad also just opened, had similar aspirations, whereupon the Gloucester & Berkeley Co. responded by admitting one and all upon payment of tolls.

Trade on the Gloucester & Cheltenham Tramroad soon created

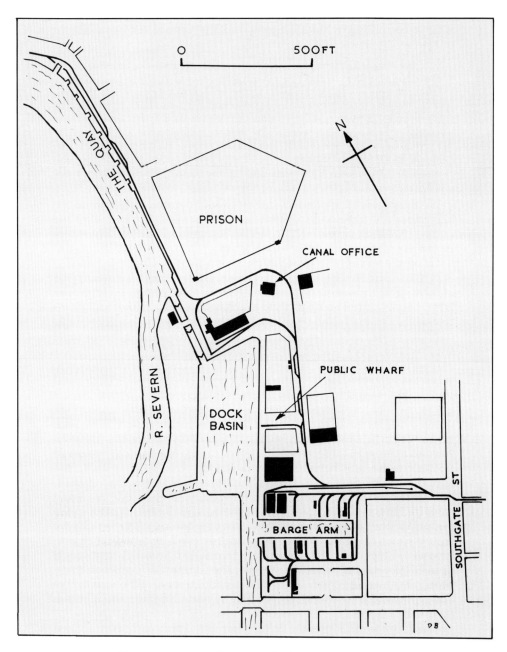

The tramroad at Gloucester docks and quay, 1843.

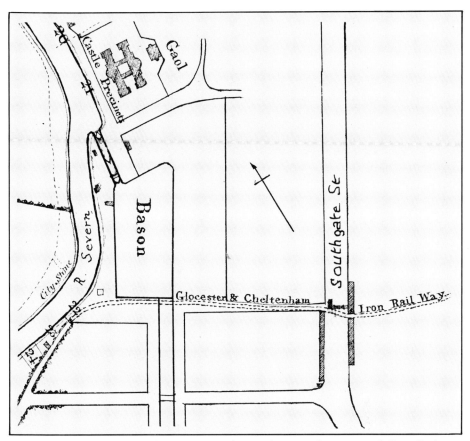

Part of Trophimus Fulljames' map of 1810 showing the tramroad (Iron Rail Way) commencing on the banks of the Severn. *GRO*

demand for a crane and jetties at the river and the canal company tried to reap a benefit by erecting gates across the line and charging tonnage. However, the illegality of the move was pointed out by Charles Newmarch, Jelf and Jones, and was quietly dropped.

In 1812 the tramroad opened the parliamentary route with eight branches leading to the edge of the basin, it now being open for river traffic. At the end of 1813 notice to remove the temporary bridge was given and not long afterwards the jetties at Naight Wharf were dismantled, though hardly before the river had done the job gratuitously.

As for the main line to Cheltenham, its opening had been expected in October 1811, but it seems that Naight Wharf had speeded up construction considerably. The official opening took place on 4th June, 1811, being accompanied by the usual jollifications.

> The important measure of a Railway or Tram Road from Gloucester to this town, having been completed on Monday evening last, the morning of Tuesday was ushered in by the ringing of bells; and about 11 o'clock a numerous assemblage of persons took place on the Railway Wharf, near the Turnpike, in order to celebrate the occasion. A train of carriages moved along the Railway, some of which were appropriately fitted up and oc-cupied by Ladies and Gentlemen, preceded by an excellent band of music; others were laden with building-stone of superior quality from Leck-hampton Hill, and coals from Gloucester. An elegant dinner was after-wards served up at the George Hotel, to a large party of gentlemen; the Hon. Mr Dutton presided on the occasion, and the evening passed off with the greatest unanimity and cordiality, everyone appearing highly gratified by the completion of a measure of such vast importance to the town of Cheltenham, and the county at large.

Hardly had the festivities subsided when serious troubles overtook Gwinnett and Benjamin Newmarch. They were joint owners of the

Benjamin Newmarch's Albion Brewery about 1826. Note part of the tram-road, bottom left.

Albion Brewery, an expensive new concern beside the tramroad depot, and a speculation which proved unprofitable. A few weeks after the line opened, Gwinnett resigned both from the brewery and the tramroad solicitors, and within a month was declared bankrupt. Later, however, he returned to the legal profession. Newmarch was unable to reverse the brewery's fortunes, and advertised it for sale. Finding no takers, he followed his partner into bankruptcy in May, 1813.

In the first year or two a very important traffic over the line consisted of stone water-pipes. These came by road from the recently opened Stone Pipe Company's works near Guiting on the Cotswolds, and thence by tramroad to the River Severn for shipment to London and Manchester. Before it crashed, this remarkable concern actually promoted a tramroad from Guiting, the Cheltenham & Cotswold Hills Railway, the story of which is told later.

The immediate consequence of the Gloucester and Cheltenham Tramroad was a rapid fall in the price of coal, the Cheltenham Coal Company announcing "at their Yard, adjoining the Railway Wharf, best coal at very reduced prices". In the following winter, best Shropshire and Forest of Dean coal was available at £1 4s. 0d. per ton. (By 1818, best quality forest of Dean coal could be had for 16/3d. per ton delivered.) Before, coal via the Coombe Hill Canal had demanded £1 15s. 1d. per ton. But the tramroad company was not satisfied with these reductions and recommended Mr Charles Kemp who was willing to sell "best Bullo Pill" at £1 2s. 6d. (The peculiar description was derived from the Bullo Pill Tramroad, opened in 1810, by which Forest of Dean coal was carried to Bullo Pill, a small dock below Newnham, from whence it came by river to Gloucester.)

The Coombe Hill Coal Company whose yard and offices were in Chester Walk, St George's Place, Cheltenham, objected to competition and determined to scuttle Mr Kemp with a cleverly worded announcement. It prompted a spirited reply in the local paper of 3rd September, 1812.

A MOST insidious ADVERTISEMENT having appeared in the last weeks Cheltenham Chronicle, and having been since industriously circulated, which if not so intended, was at least calculated to induce a belief in the Public mind, that CHARLES KEMP had given up his COAL trade to the Coombe Hill Canal Company; he therefore begs leave most positively to assure his friends and the Public

THAT HE HAD NOT, NOR EVER HAD, THE REMOTEST INTENTION OF RELINQUISHING HIS TRADE

But on the contrary, grateful for the many favours and generous support he has hitherto experienced at their hands, he is determined to continue to

Sell COAL OF THE FIRST QUALITY

at the

RAILWAY WHARF

Nevertheless, the tramroad never captured all the coal trade and for many years large tonnages reached the town via the Coombe Hill Canal. It finally closed in 1876.

The tramroad depot, where a few warehouses and lofts were still available to let "for the accommodation of persons disposed to trade on the Rail Road" was put to novel use in September 1813. It was chosen as the spot from whence a Mr Sadler would begin his "Aerial Voyage" in a hydrogen balloon. Great crowds assembled to see the ascent which it was claimed would "rise to a height of one mile and will send down a parachute with a living animal in it". However, in spite of the consumption of nearly three tons of vitriolic acid and iron filings, insufficient gas was generated to elevate the bulk of Mr Sadler, let alone the animal as well, and the crowd had to be content with the sight of Sadler junior, aged 16 years, disappearing beyond the horizon. He landed safely near Chipping Norton. These lighter moments apart, the tramroad company had unpalatable problems to discuss at its twice yearly general meeting, which was held at the George Hotel, in the High Street, Cheltenham, until the depot offices were ready in 1813.

Initially, part of the permanent way proved unsatisfactory and the company was "proceeding to relay the Road, it being on false ground". Further to these setbacks, traffic had been slow to develop and the undertaking had proved much more expensive than anticipated. The unhappy financial position culminated in 1815 in an Act, expressly obtained to raise more money (£15,000) to wipe out the debt. Together with the 1809 Act, the authorized capital was now £50,000, a figure which seems to have sufficed to cover the eventual overall cost. The pecuniary problems were now solved, at least for the present.

During this period an enterprise may be mentioned, which in the unlikely event of success could have greatly affected the tramroad's future.

The formation of a company was proposed in June 1814 to bore for coal near the line outside Cheltenham where the ground beneath the clay "which as far as has been proved, abounds with such impregnations as induce the best Mineralogists to conclude that the lower Strata must be very rich and valuable . . .". But like earlier attempts to find coal in the area, notably on Cleeve Hill (north-east of the town) the project came to nothing, doubtless to the relief of a local resident who feared that the mines would draw off all the Spa waters!

In 1819 there were two developments of lasting importance to trade on the tramroad. An Act was granted for lighting Cheltenham with gas — one of the very earliest of such commercial enterprises, and "upwards of 30 tons of iron pipes, a gazometer, and a large quantity of Stourbridge bricks" arrived at the depot. The gas works were to be on the opposite side of the Gloucester turnpike road, behind various coal wharves which had sprung up since the line opened. Sidings for coal trams were laid into the works and remained in use till about 1850 when cheaper supplies were available from the Midland Railway coal sidings some half mile away.

Much of the plant for the gas works came from the Horsley Iron Co., and its first manager was Benjamin Newmarch, now emerged from bankruptcy. One of the main suppliers was the Parkend Coal Co., and in 1821 David Mushet, the Forest of Dean ironmaster, attempted to gain a large contract. Three tons of coal came over the tramroad, probably from his mines in Bicslade near Coleford, but the trials did not prove successful. As for Newmarch, he tendered his resignation after a couple of years and then calmly offered to lease the whole concern. The gesture was declined.

The Cheltenham turnpike trustees in 1819, formed a large wharf for storing and breaking several thousand tons of Bristol stone for the roads. The wharf, at the back of the depot, was fed by a branch line for which the tramroad company received an annual rent of £5 10s. 0d. The line ran down the side of Knapp Road (now Market Street), and the site of the wharf was later built upon by the GWR Honeybourne line.

About this time another branch of similar length was laid from the Leckhampton branch to a rural stone depot and workshops known as Grottens Wharf, a large area at the junction of Norwood Road and Suffolk Road, Cheltenham. The line and depot were very probably made by Henry Norwood Trye after inheriting his father's property in 1812.

Nine years after the Gloucester and Cheltenham Tramroad opened, James, Lord Sherborne died, in May, 1820, and his estates went to his son John, who became the second Lord Sherborne. Being easily the largest shareholder he naturally took a lively interest in the company and usually attended the management meetings in Cheltenham, which involved a round trip by phaeton of thirty-five hilly Cotswold miles. Later, he also had shares in at least one other horse railway — the "Coalpit Heath Rail Road" at Bristol.

By the end of 1821, Sherborne and his colleagues introduced an important change in the methods of operating the line. They decided to lease or farm out the tolls, a practice commonly adopted by the trustees of turnpike roads and to a lesser extent by other tramroads. The lessee's task was to supervise collection of tolls and generally see to day to day matters — in other words, to do the agent's job, in exchange for an agreed payment to the company. In this way the shareholders got, at least in theory, a guaranteed dividend and the management was relieved of some of its responsibilities.

The lessee was Benjamin Newmarch, who took the office early in 1822. Before the year ended, his brother Charles, who had been clerk since the company's inception, became bankrupt and died a few months later, on 10th January, 1823. Sherborne recorded in his diaries "a good man and attached to my interests though not altogether a good agent. But in him I have lost a confidential adviser and an upright clearheaded friend".

Benjamin Newmarch leased the tolls for about five years and during the period became associated with some abortive trials of a steam locomotive on the tramroad. He had also colliery interests in the Forest of Dean. The heavy traffic over the line is reflected in the toll permits issued at Gloucester alone; 6279 between 26th January, 1824 and 19th January, 1825, corresponding to an average load of perhaps 4 tons each.

Late in 1825 Newmarch also leased the tolls of the Kingsholm and Wotton turnpike gates at Gloucester, and a year later the weighing machines were let to the Gloucester and Cheltenham Railway Co. The reason for such an involvement is obscure. The company reverted to the old system when Newmarch's lease expired, and Thomas Royce became agent until his death in February 1828.

Shortly afterwards, Newmarch again stepped into the job but before long had once more descended into financial trouble. George Newmarch wrote to the long suffering Sherborne giving "a bad account of his Brother Ben's affairs and urging me to apply again to the Duke of Wellington for something for his Brother Joseph". Clearly the Newmarches were a considerable liability. Lord Sherborne, however, soon had even more to worry about for, in March, 1829, he described the tramroad company as ". . . a very unpromising concern — no chance of a dividend at present". Things were no better fifteen months later. The line was still "a very bad concern" and in debt to the tune of £10,000. One is tempted to conclude that the affairs of Benjamin and the company were not entirely unconnected.

However, the crisis did not prevent the appearance of another steam locomotive, the *Royal William*, about the end of 1831. Whether Newmarch promoted these trials is not known, though the Gloucester & Berkeley Canal records reveal that he was still very closely involved in the tramroad. (The story of the experiments with locomotives is told in Chapter 6.)

During the 1830s property development in both Gloucester and Cheltenham surrounded much of the tramroad. In the city, St James' Place (now Park Road) was built beside the line and a tramroad depot and coalyard of considerable size was located at its junction with Parker's Row (now Brunswick Road). The depot, sometimes called Spa Wharf after the ill-fated spa nearby, existed before 1825 and later became the company's headquarters. One or two of the old buildings are still there, on the edge of the yard which now serves as a private car-park.

In Cheltenham, the route from Westall Green to the Leckhampton Road was likewise flanked with dwellings. H.N. Trye's branch to Grotten's Wharf gave way to Great Norwood Street and was replaced by two long sidings on ground occupied until recently by Parry's woodyard. It is now a housing development. This area became the new Grotten's Wharf.

A short distance up the line sidings diverged into a large coalyard bordering Grafton Street on its north side, and extending to Bath Road.

By the mid-1830s coal traffic had levelled out at around 25,000 tons per year. Dividends of 6–7 per cent were being paid, but the years were taking their toll of the old brigade; Sir William Hicks died in October, 1934, Benjamin Newmarch in December, and Captain Thomas Gray in May, 1835.

Before Newmarch's death at the early age of 49, Lord Sherborne consulted him about a successor. A Mr Henry Lucy was being considered, but in spite of misgivings on the part of Newmarch he gained the position. Lucy was a builder and surveyor who had established himself in Cheltenham by 1820 and throughout his life seems to have emulated the financial instability of his predecessor. Although officially agent, he often acted as clerk, yet found time to run his old trade on the side, into the path of which, on suitable occasions, his new post enabled lucrative business to be directed.

As an example of how closely interwoven were the personalities of various major concerns in those days, Stephen Ballard, the Hereford and Gloucester Canal engineer and later a well known railway contractor, became apprenticed to Henry Lucy as a young man in 1825. The training was never completed due to a periodic Lucy crash, but it put Ballard in good stead. He remembered his old master and often put work his way.

Lucy arrived in time to see the end of an era. Great changes were taking place in the environment of the tramroad, and the old order was soon to be supplanted. Horse railways were often physically and economically in the path of the new steam lines and many were purchased only to be buried, sometimes literally.

We shall presently see how the tramroad company was bought up, but no one, least of all its new owners, could have believed that the old line would serve for another twenty-five years.

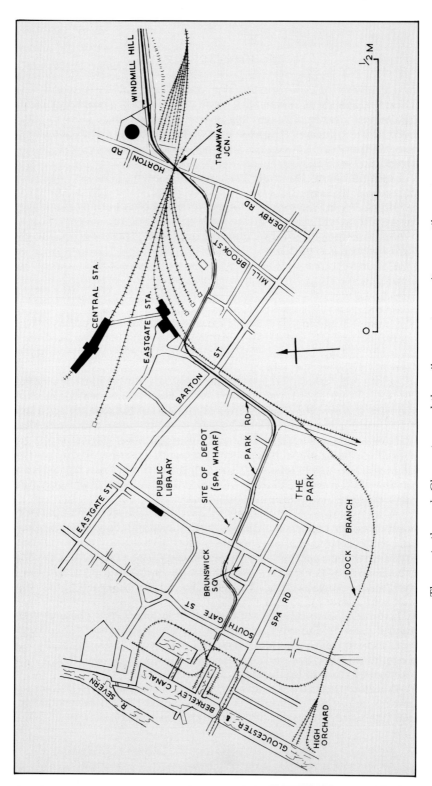

The route through Gloucester, and the railway system as it was until recent years. Eastgate Station and the Docks Branch are now closed.

Chapter Three
Under New Management

The latter half of the tramroad's life span when it belonged to the new steam railways is complicated. It suffered several changes of ownership, brought about by peculiar circumstances between 1836 and 1845 and to confuse matters further, the new owners were themselves bought out.

The tramroad shares were held by trustees who were also directors of the owning companies and at times Gilbertian situations occurred in which the former were virtually at loggerheads with their own railway boards.

The murmurings of these developments were first manifest in the 1820s when, situated between the important manufacturing city of Birmingham and the port of Bristol, the tramroad found itself involved in the country's growing railway system.

As early as 1824 or 1825, proposals were under way for a line linking the two cities and, according to I.K. Brunel, they included the tramroad in the route. These ideas faded, but the success of the Gloucester and Berkeley Canal, opened in 1827, encouraged their revision in 1833, although in a less ambitious form, as the Birmingham and Gloucester Railway. This line would enable Birmingham freight to be carried partly by rail and partly by water, with transshipment at Gloucester for Bristol, coastal and export markets.

Captain W.S. Moorsom was the promoter's engineer and he chose a direct line via the village of Boddington to Gloucester docks, avoiding Cheltenham altogether. Then, after two years, second thoughts prevailed. The course was revised nearer the town and crossed the Cheltenham–Gloucester road by the Pheasant Inn, terminating at a passenger station near Gloucester gaol. A short branch was included to Cheltenham with another leaving the main line about half a mile from the terminus and leading to the canal a little way below the docks. The area was known as High Orchard, and here the company proposed to build a basin and depot.

At the same time, 1835, the broad gauge Cheltenham and Great Western Union Railway was mooted, from the town via Gloucester to meet the projected Great Western Railway at Swindon. H.N. Trye was acting-chairman, and five of its directors were also members of the provisional committee of the Birmingham and Gloucester Railway.

In spite of this connection, relations between the two parties were sometimes strained. Each was anxious to get the tramroad traffic and possibly the line itself, for although the Birmingham and Gloucester Railway had dropped the impractical idea of converting the tramroad to their standard gauge, they saw logic in acquiring it, if only for

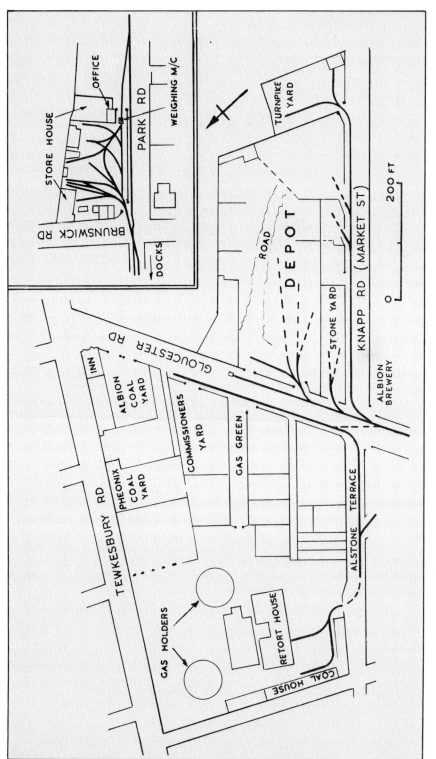

The tramroad terminus in Cheltenham, and inset, the Spa Wharf and offices in Park Road, Gloucester, 1851.

access to the docks; in fact the Cheltenham and Great Western Union already had an eye on this latter possibility, and in November, 1835, an advertisement concerning their Parliamentary Bill announced the intention of contracting with the tramroad company "for the alteration of the line of Tramroad . . . to construct a Railway thereon".

Believing in attack as the best form of defence, the Cheltenham company then accused the Birmingham and Gloucester of wishing to buy the tramroad but it was claimed that they had "never entertained the idea" and the Birmingham company added that no such attempt would be made without first informing them.

Nevertheless, Samuel Bowly of the Birmingham and Gloucester quietly met Lord Sherborne and George Newmarch early in January, 1836, but with no positive result. A row now arose between the suitors, after which the Birmingham and Gloucester felt morally able to act exclusively for its own interests. Bowly therefore tried again, on 18th January, and approached Lord Suffolk who was probably deputising for Lord Sherborne. As a result of the interview, Bowly "conceived his Lordship would be desposed to recommend the acceptance of £30,000 in cash", and a decision was taken to agree to the terms at the next tramroad meeting on 28th January. However, a snubbing letter from George Newmarch was received, stating that the presence of the Birmingham and Gloucester party would be inconvenient — the Cheltenham and Great Western Union were to be present with a higher offer!

Afterwards, Lord Sherborne wrote of the meeting "Hyett and Stevens [sic] came and agreed to give £35,000 and we consented to take it".

He must have been well satisfied with the deal.

Meanwhile a sudden rapprochement between the rivals had occurred and on the very next day they resolved to come to an agreement about various matters including the joint purchase of the tramroad and building a common line between Cheltenham and Gloucester. It is significant that Stephens was one of the five associated with both new companies.

The takeover was conditional on each company getting its Act, and payment had to be made within the following six months. These conditions being fulfilled in due course, the new owners' first task was to appoint trustees for the tramroad's management. Early in 1837, each company elected three representatives, Messrs. John Chadborn, William Washbourn and William Seale Evans of the Birmingham and Gloucester, and W.H. Hyett, Charles Stephens and Thomas Griffiths of the Cheltenham and Great Western Union. Griffiths by the way, held a partnership with Charles Laurence of

Cirencester; they were solicitors to the latter company, the GWR, and also by this time, to the tramroad company.

The new committee seems to have made few, if any, changes in staff employed by the tramroad. Henry Lucy remained as agent and his duties were roughly those of general manager. During his years in office (1834–1842) traffic on the line was heavy, averaging about sixty tram journeys per day in each direction. In 1838, it amounted to over 35,000 tons of coal, road stone and sundries to which must be added nearly 23,000 tons (probably mainly Cotswold stone) carried over the Leckhampton branch.

This same year saw construction work advancing on the Birmingham and Gloucester railway. At Cheltenham, its route passed under the Gloucester turnpike road and the tramroad just before the site chosen for the new Lansdown station. Close by, the tramroad branch left the main route at "Leckhampton Junction" where a tramroad toll house, weighing machine and garden stood in isolation. This little group obstructed a half mile grand approach (Queens Road) which the Birmingham and Gloucester company were to build alongside the tramroad branch from Westall Green to the station and to the turnpike road beyond; it therefore had to go. The tramroad company was paid £140 for the site, Lucy arranging for the demolition soon afterwards. The Lansdown and Westall Green district was then being developed by its landowner, Pearson Thompson, who had earlier been on the provisional committee of the Birmingham and Gloucester Railway. He sold the ground for the new road for £500, construction of which cost the company £220 6s. 0d. The road was later allowed to lapse into a deplorable condition and was not taken over by the Town Commissioners until the early 1860s.

Since the tramroad passed very close to the site chosen for the station, a plan came out in September, 1839, to reduce the disadvantage of its remoteness from the town (over a mile from the centre). The idea was to lay a standard gauge branch for coal wagons along the tramroad to the depot, but it did not go beyond the proposal stage.

The chance of a little private business had not escaped Mr Lucy, who just before the station came into use in June, 1840, presented a Bill to the Birmingham and Gloucester company for re-routing and relaying the tramroad over the new bridge across the railway. After several interviews in which the cost of another job was allowed, he received £98 4s. 0d. for the work.

In August, 1840, the tramroad underwent a further change in ownership, the Birmingham and Gloucester company gaining complete control. To learn how this came about we must revert to 1837, when the Cheltenham and Great Western Union had already got itself into serious difficulties. The Birmingham and Gloucester naturally grew concerned as to probable delays in building the common line and therefore obtained an Act in 1838 for powers to buy the Cheltenham company's share of work done and then to finish it themselves. They were also entitled to purchase the half share which the Cheltenham company held in the tramroad.

Arising from these powers, new names appeared amongst the tramroad trustees and management committee, which thenceforth comprised Messrs. Washbourn, Evans, Samuel Bowly, R. Canning and Samuel Baker of Highnam Court near Gloucester, all of whom were directors of the Birmingham and Gloucester Railway.

Soon afterwards, in November, 1840, the Birmingham and Gloucester line opened throughout to the Gloucester terminus, at a site near the present station and about 250 yards from the tramroad.

The railway's arrival might have been expected to precipitate a sharp fall in the tramroad's fortunes, but this was not so. Its revenue, being mainly derived from coal, was hardly affected, because the new line could not compete. In the first year or two the Birmingham and Gloucester did try bringing Midlands coal to Cheltenham, but the cost of carriage and the remoteness of the line from the town rendered the initial experiment a failure. Forest of Dean coal was very popular in Cheltenham, and this it was quite unable to carry without rail access to the Gloucester and Berkeley canal, and in any event to poach such trade from the tramroad, then still paying good dividends, would have been tantamount to cutting off its nose to spite its face.

The real incentive behind the Birmingham company's desire to reach the canal was, of course, Birmingham–Bristol and coastal traffic, and only when this was attained in 1848 did coal trade on the tramroad fall drastically.

The story of this interesting period when the tramroad became thickly involved in its owners' continually frustrated efforts to get to the canal and how it acted as carrier for the traffic will now be related.

As will have been gathered, the High Orchard branch originally proposed in 1836 had not materialised. As a substitute the Birmingham and Gloucester company proposed in 1839 to apply for powers to build a branch from the station to High Orchard, in which part of the route would run beside the tramroad in Park Road. However, Worcester, jealous of her Severn trade, did not favour the idea, and succeeded in getting the Bill withdrawn.

Not to be outdone, the Birmingham and Gloucester announced that "arrangements are in progress whereby the extension to the canal may be attained without the intervention of Parliament". These arrangements were tried soon after the railway opened and turned out to be a Heath Robinson scheme whereby the tramroad, passing near the station on its way to the docks, was to be altered to enable railway wagons to run over it, or if this failed, "a carriage might be constructed which could travel on the curves of the tramway when thus altered". Although experiments were apparently made for several months, the result was, needless to say, abortive.

The Birmingham and Gloucester company then came firmly down to earth and decided to use the tramroad in its proper role. The necessary 250 yard spur from the main line of tramroad was completed into the station on 23rd August, 1841. Trans-shipment of goods from wagons to trams was, of course, necessary and, together with the cost and inconvenience of working the rail-water traffic over the tramroad, this temporary solution was hardly satisfactory. Nevertheless, the old line had come in useful at last.

Still anxious for a solution, we find that in September, 1842, the Birmingham and Gloucester Railway was thinking of straddling the tramroad in Park Road with its rails, en route to High Orchard. This objective was becoming increasingly desirable, for £14,000 had already been spent there on the basin, warehouses and coke ovens and the company was shortly to be heavily criticized for "this very injudicious outlay". But it was also aware that as the tramroad had been authorized by Act of Parliament, it could not be altered indiscriminately. A Mr A.W. Daniel, who had recently appeared amongst the trustees, was asked to report under the heading "Power of this Company over the Tramway". His conclusion must have been favourable, for a decision was taken to apply for powers to go ahead, but the Bill failed to pass the Standing Orders Committee.

The Birmingham and Gloucester now turned to another scheme, in which for some reason High Orchard was altogether omitted. The docks were to be gained by a junction from the main line, half a mile before the station, where it crossed the tramroad. With suitable easing of curves, the branch would straddle the tramroad apart from the last 100 yards where a direct route took the rails over Southgate Street.

At this stage, the position was complicated by a not unexpected development. The Cheltenham and Great Western Union had been progressively going down the hill and in July 1843, was bought out by the GWR. The GWR also claimed the right, allowed by the 1838 Act, to repurchase a half share in both the common line between Gloucester and Cheltenham, and the tramroad company, but it did not exercise these powers for the present.

Meanwhile traffic over the tramroad between the Birmingham & Gloucester station and the docks increased to the point where its inadequacies were becoming intolerable. In particular, wool could not be carried because of its great bulk and the restricted loading gauge. Thus in September 1843 the idea of straddling the lines with standard gauge rails revived, the estimated cost being £707 for just over 2000 yards in length. To this end the Birmingham & Gloucester solicited the tramroad trustees for support, which was forthcoming on the understanding that they would be indemnified against any possible legal actions.

But a further complication arose in the form of the broad-gauge lobby. Construction of the Swindon–Gloucester line was advancing rapidly with assistance from the GWR, the new station being adjacent to the Birmingham & Gloucester terminus. In the light of these developments the Birmingham & Gloucester deemed it prudent to consult the GWR on their dock access plans and I.K. Brunel came down to Gloucester to examine them in January 1844. As a result the GWR gave its blessing on condition that standard gauge rails alone should not accompany the tramroad, but broad gauge also! The operating difficulties combined with mechanical complexities at points and crossings no doubt became apparent on reflection, and nothing more was heard of the great man's proposition.

Having obtained Counsel's opinion confirming the legality of the scheme, the Birmingham & Gloucester determined to press ahead. However, the GWR, having an interest in the old line, insisted that traffic upon it would be largely destroyed, and filed a short Bill of Injunction. The case finally went before the Lord Chancellor before ending in the GWR's defeat, the business being extensively reported in the *Gloucester Journal* 20th April and 4th May, 1844. The reasons behind the GWR's tenacity are difficult to explain.

In the summer the broad gauge station at Gloucester was opened to receive another line, the Bristol & Gloucester Railway, but its impact on trade via the canal was not very marked.

The way was now clear and about the end of May 1844 standard gauge rails at last reached the docks. This presumably brought to an end the use of the tramroad for ferrying goods, but by an arrangement with the Birmingham & Gloucester the trustees received 6d./ton tolls, apparently regardless of the mode of conveyance.

Traffic over the tramroad to Cheltenham still continued largely undiminished, and with standard gauge goods as well the level-crossing in Southgate Street must have been almost permanently closed to road vehicles. In the year ending April 1845 no less than 45,000 tons were thus conveyed between docks and station, not counting tramroad trade to Cheltenham, all of which was pulled by horses.

Besides these problems, the white elephant at High Orchard was proving an increasing embarrassment to the Birmingham and Gloucester Railway who now, independently of the GWR, proposed to submit to Parliament a more ambitious plan than any yet conceived.

It included the usual line along the tramroad to the docks, with the addition of a branch to High Orchard, and for good measure extensions were also proposed to High Orchard and even considered to the west of the docks. Whilst these plans were in the pipeline, the Birmingham and Gloucester suffered a fate comparable to its late companion, the Cheltenham and Great Western Union, and was absorbed by the Midland Railway in January, 1845. The takeover did not affect the Bill and an Act of Parliament was at last achieved in June, 1845.

Nevertheless, having gained these somewhat extravagant powers, the Midland applied no urgency to their execution. Rails to High Orchard and the main dock basin were not completed until 1848 and the route ignored the tramroad completely, leaving it to work out its declining years in peace.

Having, and not without a certain sigh of relief, concluded our account of the long struggle to gain the docks, something must be said of the men who steered the Gloucester & Cheltenham Railway Co. through the midst of such a political and generally fraught period.

Henry Lucy continued as manager, but in August 1842 created consternation by absconding to America with £432 of the tramroad's cash in his pocket. This seemingly inexcusable liberty was, however, ameliorated by the discovery of a document in his desk which made over property to the extent of the loss. Indeed, within a year he was back and working for the old firm, though in a lesser role. How long the job lasted is not known, and Lucy was last heard of in 1852 in an unusual legal case involving the building of Cheltenham's General Hospital, of which he was Clerk to the Works.

Faced with Lucy's dramatic exit, the company needed a replacement and Samuel Baker, the management committee chairman, brought forward a Mr Charles Church as having been elected as the new "superintendent" subject to the approval of the Birmingham and Gloucester Railway. He may have been the Charles Church who was on the Gloucester and Berkeley committee many years previously.

Church was in his 68th year but "felt himself fully competent to perform and willingly to undertake the duties of the office". He gained the post in spite of the Birmingham company's regret that the trustees were unable to find a younger man.

About this time, the tramroad management seems to have shifted from Cheltenham to Gloucester, but Church, a Gloucester man, had a certain amount of tramroad business in Cheltenham and was allowed a free pass on the railway until January 1843, after which he had to pay.

In common with his predecessors Church was something of a character, as may be gathered from an incident in March 1845.

Just outside Gloucester, the Birmingham & Gloucester, Bristol and Gloucester and GWR lines converged and crossed the tramroad together, at the appropriately named Tramway Crossing. At this spot was also Horton Road level-crossing, and these busy gates were kept by a Birmingham & Gloucester employee, Michael Moseley.

With three railways, a road, and a horse-operated plateway all converging at one point, his job cannot have been easy. Whether due to delays to tramroad traffic or some other cause is not certain, but Church and Moseley fell out, Church ending up on a charge of assault. He was fined 10/- plus costs, but told the magistrates that he "would do the same again".

Such belligerence displeased the Birmingham & Gloucester, who "expressed to the tramroad committee the surprise of the Board at the extraordinary conduct of Mr Church." We may suspect that Church was not without sympathisers and perhaps friends in the local press, for nothing of the incident ever appeared in print. Church continued as "superintendent of the line", and in 1851 lived at No. 1 London Road, Gloucester (long since demolished), with his daughter Hannah, aged 33, and two servants. His situation as manager of the Gloucester & Cheltenham Tramroad was not without reward.

We will now turn attention to the final years of the tramroad, but before so doing, must record a final change in its ownership. We have seen how, arising from the consequences of the 1838 Act, the GWR was empowered to repurchase a half share in both the Gloucester–Cheltenham common line, and in the tramroad. They exercised these rights in 1845, after which the old line was equally managed by themselves and the Midland Railway.

The tramroad's last decade is the story of a long drawn out decline. Traffic gradually fell as the Midland opened wharves in Cheltenham for Staffordshire, Derbyshire and Shropshire coal and at an increasing rate when the High Orchard branch encouraged a direct erosion of trade. The opening of the South Wales Railway, allowing uninterrupted rail access after July, 1854, from the Forest of Dean to Cheltenham, was almost the final blow, but a little coal was still conveyed over the line until the end, by quarry trams returning to Leckhampton after delivering their burden to the docks.

With the rail branch completed, the Cheltenham Town Commissioners and Turnpike Trustees realized that the Midland Railway should be better able to carry their stone; however, new wharves would be needed and like the coal wharves, these would not be so convenient, for the tramroad enabled stone to be deposited where required on the Gloucester–Cheltenham road and also to reach the south part of the town, where *Grottens Wharf* was used for its reception. Stone traffic therefore continued and, in so doing, kept the line going for some years.

Meanwhile, Charles Church did his best to cut overheads to a minimum. In April, 1852, the tramroad company was summoned for 17s. rates due to Staverton parish, and Church, in objecting to pay, claimed that the line had lost all its profits and nearly all its traffic. In September, 1853, he appealed against the rates levied by the adjacent parish of Boddington, but the case was dismissed due to his absence, ironically because of a late train. However, three months later he got a reduction in gross value from £44 15s. 4d. to £9 10s. 0d.

After 1854, income only barely exceeded expenditure and soon the tramroad was reckoned to be a nuisance in both Cheltenham and Gloucester. Its tracks, running unguarded along miles of streets and verges, caused hazards to pedestrians and road vehicles and complaints of cruelty to the horses were common. In Cheltenham, the Commissioners asserted that the rails were in a bad state and here and there derelict trams lay scattered beside the line.

By 1858 the tramroad owners and the local authorities agreed that the line must go. However, attempts were made to retain the Leckhampton branch from Trye's quarries to the Gloucester Road, but local opposition was too strong and "The Gloucester and Cheltenham Tramroads Abandonment Act" was obtained on 1st August, 1859. It specified that the line must be disposed of within two years and portions of the route were to be handed over to the Cheltenham Town Commissioners to allow road and other improvements to be carried out.

The Act obliged the Midland Railway and the GWR (which by this time had access to the west side of Gloucester docks) to carry Bristol stone to Cheltenham for agreed charges. The lowest rates were for material for the turnpike road and directly resulted from the tramroad Act of 1809 which provided for its toll-free carriage.

However, the Act having been obtained, neither the Railways nor the Cheltenham authorities seemed so anxious to implement it, but a site at the GWR St James station was eventually chosen for reception of the stone. In March, 1861, the GWR, aware that time was running out, found it necessary to write the following ultimatum to the surveyor of the Cheltenham Turnpike Trustees, Mr J.H. McIlquham.

> Great Western Railway,
> Cirencester.
> 4th March, 1861

Dear Sir,

We are informed some objection has been raised to the breaking up of the Tramroad in consequence of some new Depot for Stone not having been provided at Cheltenham.

The Tramroad Company is actually dissolved from the passing of the Act and the Midland and Great Western Companies are enjoined by the Act (of which every one is bound to take notice) to stop up and abandon the Tramroad. This cannot be any longer delayed . . . Understanding you are the Surveyor to the trustees of the Roads, we beg to inform you that instructions have been given to the Engineer to break up the Plates on the 18th of this Month.

We are dear Sir,

> Your very obedient Servant,
> Charles and C.W. Laurence

Charles Church, although now at 86 a very old man, probably arranged for the sale of the line by a local auctioneer, Mr Knowles, and the date chosen was 19th April, 1861.

Most of the plates went to Forest of Dean buyers, one purchasing over 600 tons. The cast iron plates fetched 58s. per ton and the wrought iron over four guineas. These figures contributed almost the entire value of the sale, altogether £2,703, a figure which was considered to be highly satisfactory. The stone blocks were no doubt virtually given away. The Cheltenham depot was sold separately on 9th July, 1861, and ten days later the Gloucester depot, where the auction took place, was also disposed of.

This, then, was the end of the Gloucester and Cheltenham Tramroad, an enterprise born of local necessity and one which fulfilled an indispensable need for many years. But one short length of the line survived until the 1890s, and the story of this remnant is described in Chapter 7.

After the line closed the Midland Railway remembered one old platelayer, Thomas Niblett, "who had been employed on the Cheltenham and Gloucester Tramway for 52 years and whose services are no longer required". They proposed to pension him off for life at 4s. per week if the GWR would make the same allowance. Let us hope they did.

Chapter Four

Permanent Way and Rolling Stock

In the past, trains have run on rails of two basic types, the edge-rail which is now universal, and the plate-rail, having an L-shaped section. This form, where the flange is on the rail instead of the wheel, has long been extinct but in Southern Britain virtually ousted its rival in the period 1800–1820. For horse-drawn traffic it was superior, enabling the construction of much lighter wagons due to the great saving in weight consequent upon use of narrow wheels without the broad treads necessary on edge rails. Savings of up to half a ton might thus be achieved.

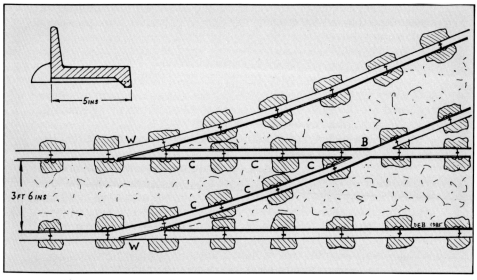

Details of a Turnout, and section of a tramplate. B, Box plate; C, Channel plate; W, Wing plate.

A drawback was a tendency for the plates to clog with stones and debris. Furthermore due to an uneconomical section, they tended to fracture unless of a very heavy pattern. These limitations were however tolerated as long as horse-power held sway.

In the 1820s very early scientific trials were made to determine rolling resistance on a number of railways including the Gloucester & Cheltenham. The instigator was Henry Palmer of the Institution of Civil Engineers, with the aim of furthering his recently invented monorail system. The results given below have been abstracted from Galloway's *History and Progress of the Steam Engine.*

	Railway	Material Conveyed	Rollability
1.	Cheltenham Tram Road	Coal	1 in 90
12.	New Branch of ditto, slightly covered in dust	Coal	1 in 122
3.	Ditto, swept clean	Coal	1 in 146
4.	Surrey Tram Road	Chalk	1 in 60
5.	Llanelly Tram Road	Coal	1 in 59
6.	Edge Rail Road near Newcastle	Coal	1 in 170
7.	Penrhyn Edge Rail Road, Curved Surface	Slate	1 in 87
8.	Palmer's Railway	Coal	1 in 300

The Gloucester & Cheltenham was clearly the best plateway, though the reasons are uncertain. Interesting though they were, the tests did not prove a great deal, except that rollability was not of sole importance — Palmer's idea in the end proved a failure.

It has been claimed that plateways permitted the use of road carts, thus providing a very flexible transport system. But if certain historians thought so, contemporary opinion did not, because except in one or two special instances the gauge was always too narrow. Furthermore, carts were of too small a capacity to take much advantage of an iron road.

The permanent way of the Gloucester & Cheltenham Tramroad conformed to the usual practice of the period. The gauge measured 3ft 6in. between the inner sides of the flanges, a figure which must have been settled by C.B. Trye's lines already on Leckhampton Hill. Although rather narrow, it was a favourite with Hodgkinson; he later built several lines in the Forest of Dean and the Welsh Border to this dimension. Three feet long cast iron plate rails of about 46 lb. weight were employed and may have come from Hill and Hopkins' Blaenavon Ironworks or Samuel Hewlett's Ayleford Foundry near Blakeney. These companies supplied iron for tramroad branches in the early years at Gloucester docks.

Stone sleeper blocks supported the plates, which were held down by an iron spike driven into a wooden plug in each block. Plate stability was improved by an integral lug or toe at each end.

At level crossings the flanges were not permitted to rise more than an inch above the road surface and usually displayed an undulating or serrated edge to prevent carts and wagons side-slipping. Such plates, termed "Vandyke Rails", were sometimes cast with a channel section.

The permanent way of many early tramroads was not equal to the task and the Gloucester & Cheltenham had plenty of trouble in this respect, mostly with broken plates. In 1844 Charles Church wrote to the Stratford & Moreton Tramway Co. for details of their permanent way, without, however, much useful result. Wrought iron was tried at Leckhampton in quite long lengths but on the main line 3 ft cast-iron plates endured to the end. Some tramroads adopted iron chairs or even iron cross-sleepers to hold the gauge, but it does not appear that such concessions to progress ever found their way to Gloucester or Cheltenham.

As for the plates themselves, numerous complete or broken examples have been unearthed over the years, mainly at Leck-hampton where the lines worked until 1924. Some had worn right through. A full record of discoveries made some twenty years ago may be found in *Industrial Archaeology* (see Bibliography).

Most of the plates found on the course of the main line are very similar in form, which may be termed the standard Gloucester & Cheltenham pattern. It was later adopted by the Hay Tramroad and its quite sophisticated design reflects the amount of effort put into improving a fundamentally weak rail. The outcome was a hogged flange and extra stiffening under the tread, albeit on the wrong side for much benefit. The plate ends were curved in plan view, perhaps to improve lateral location, and a general similarity with the earlier Surrey Iron Railway suggests a possible ancestry. Leckhampton Hill plates exhibit many variations, no doubt reflecting second-hand sources and the whims of the quarry lessees. Weights range from 42 to 63 lbs. Altogether, the plates can be divided into seven types, apart from serrated and channelled forms used at road crossings.

Number found	Ends	Underside	Flange	Tread	Notes
1	Square	Flat	Parallel	Plain	Leckhampton
1	Square	Relieved	Parallel	Plain	Leckhampton
2	Square	Flat	Hogged	Plain	Leckhampton
1	Square	Relieved	Hogged	Plain	Leckhampton
1	Curved	Flat	Hogged	Plain	Leckhampton
2	Curved	Flat	Hogged	Stiffened	Leckhampton
6	Curved	Relieved	Hogged	Stiffened	Standard G & C

Tramplates often displayed letters cast underneath, which usually denoted owner or founder. On one Leckhampton example HNT must refer to Henry Norwood Trye, who inherited his father's estate in 1811. Other specimens bear the marks 1C, BNC and C–WCo, the doubtful letter being R, B or H. There is hardly a doubt that other tramplates will turn up from time to time, for by no means all the Leckhampton tracks were lifted, and we can be pretty sure the same applies to numerous sidings and turnouts on the main line.

Two Gloucester & Cheltenham plates together with examples from the Forest of Dean tramroads are on view at the Dean Forest Railway Preservation Society's Steam Centre at Norchard, near Lydney.

The wrought-iron nails holding the plates down were very distinctive, having a wedge-shaped rectangular head ½ in x 1¼ in., the length varying from 2½ to 4 in. Much scope remains for the study of plateway track, for this was once the commonest form of permanent way in Southern Britain.

In respect of that other essential ingredient of the line, stone blocks, we find that on 6th July, 1809, the company were advertising for "Persons willing to contract for the furnishing of BLOCKS — stating the terms on which they will deliver the Blocks per ton, upon the Quay at Gloucester, each Block not to exceed 200, nor less than 160 lb. weight".

Gloucester was probably chosen to encourage tenders from the Forest of Dean where hard sandstone was available; much of the line was laid with this material and incredibly, such blocks found their way to the tramroads on the highest part of Leckhampton Hill. However, Cotswold stone was not altogether excluded. A long stretch was revealed on the formation of the main line at Benhall near Cheltenham, whilst excavating a trench in 1964.

Laying the blocks with the holes already bored at the correct levels and spacings was a matter of no little skill, especially at passing loops, and when, in September 1813, the company requested tenders for "Forest Blocks", they also advertised for a "good block-layer".

Plateways were usually gravelled ("ballast" is a later term) up to or even over the top of the blocks and after grass had grown where it could, the casual observer saw little of the track other than two flanged rows of iron with the driver's path on each side and the horse's in the middle. In urban areas where the line ran through streets, the space between the plates was usually paved.

Hodgkinson's "Estimate of an intended Railway from Cheltenham to Gloucester" dated 30 September 1808 gives further details about the mode of construction of the line; here it is:

Purchase of 30 Acres of Land at £50 per Acre	1,500
Forming the Road 12 feet in Width on the surface, exclusive of Slopes and Drains, from Cheltenham to Gloucester being 15,800 Yards lineal at 3s. pr. Yd.	2,370
Covering the Surface of the Ground formed with Gravel or Stone broken small Six Inches in thickness on 15,800 Yards at 2s. pr. Yard	1,580
Providing Stone Blocks of 160 lb. weight each boring, beding and laying the same on the Bed of Stone, filling between and	

backing the sides with Gravel or Stone broken small, finding
Oak plugs, wrought Iron Nails on 15,800 Yds. at 4s.   ...   3,160
Passing places four in each Mile of Sixty Yards each or 2,160
Yards at 4s.   432
Culverts, Soughs, pitching the Crossings of public and Occu-
pation Roads   660
Fencing in some places on each side, occupation Gates for the
whole road   1,185
Purchase of 700 Tons of dark Grey cast Iron rails delivered on
the Line of Railway at £9 per Ton   6,300
Incidental Agency, etc. 1,818 14

                                                          £19,005 14

The corresponding estimate for the Leckhampton branch brought
the total to £25,261 14s. 0d. Hodgkinson allowed 3s. per yard for
"forming the road" for both the main line and branch, in spite of the
virtual absence of earthworks on the latter. £50 per acre for the
ground, however, was a serious error. The comparative price for the
Hay Railway, where the land was poorer, amounted to £120, and
points strongly towards a reason for the high cost of the line.

Further details of constructional costs are given in a contract dated
9th March, 1824, between Hugh McIntosh and the Berkeley Canal
Co., for laying 64 yards of tramroad at the Barge Arm. The estimate
reveals the sum at somewhat less than £1 per yard, over half the total
being due to the metals (plates).

	£	s.	d.
128 metals at 50 lb. each at £12 per ton	34	5	8
128 blocks at 1s. 6d.	9	12	0
Boring 128 blocks at 2d.	1	1	4
128 nails at 1d.		10	8
128 plugs at 1s. for 20		6	5
Laying 64 yd at 4d. per yd	1	1	0
Excavating 64 yd at 1s. 6d. per yd	4	16	0
Stoning under the road (track) and gravelling at 2s. per yd	6	8	0
	58	1	1

Hodgkinson proposed four passing places per mile on the main
line, each no less than 60 yards long. In practice, they were usually
considerably shorter, and, at least in the lines' later years, were much
more frequent. The Leckhampton branch had up to eight per mile
from 20 to 40 yards in length, at quite erratic intervals. Similar den-
sities applied to the main line in other urban areas. Extra passing
places were probably added as trade increased; indeed, in the mid
1840s, when traffic over the line in Gloucester reached a peak, most of

the route was doubled between the docks and the tramroad depot in Park Road.

On some lines, notably the Kington Tramroad in Herefordshire, where a gradual change in direction was required, the route was often engineered in straight lines, arranged as a series of chords within an imaginary arc. Passing loops were positioned where contiguous chords met to allow drivers to see if the line was clear before venturing forth. This principle seems to have applied on the Gloucester & Cheltenham Tramroad near the Pheasant Inn at Staverton, and is indicated by the course of the main road. Unfortunately it has been forgotten by modern highway engineers.

The 1809 Act specified that the width of land taken for the route should not exceed 24 feet though more was allowed for passing places, embankments, wharves etc. Judging by the few places where a double hedged boundary survives, the usual width was about 20 feet, but in one case, where the line passed through George Caesar Hopkinson's property in Pound Lane (now Elmbridge Road, Gloucester), it was restricted to 6 feet, excluding fences.

Where the route ran beside the turnpike road, the Act required that their centre distances must be less than 30 feet apart and any unwanted land between road and tramroad boundaries, if less than 20 feet wide, had to be bought and laid open to the road. This provided an incentive to keep the two close together, unless a worthwhile short cut could be taken, and explains why much of the route has disappeared in road widening operations.

The gradients on the main line were confined to the vicinity of Gloucester, and near Cheltenham. Leaving the docks, the route climbed at about 1 in 180 to the depot in Park Road and with a similar grade from Barton Street to Horton Road (Tramway Crossing). Beyond, it ran virtually level to Staverton Bridge, where a three mile ascent commenced to the summit at Lansdown Castle, the last mile of which was at a steady 1 in 100. The final mile to the Cheltenham depot ran slightly downhill.

The Leckhampton branch to the foot of the inclines was much more severely graded, averaging 1 in 70. The course ran entirely uphill, steepening to approximately 1 in 35 over the last few hundred yards.

Apart from Trye's small and rather primitive quarry trams, virtually nothing is known of those which covered countless unrecorded journeys between Gloucester and Cheltenham. This is a pity, because some were unusually large for a 3ft 6in. gauge line. An old man who died in 1934 described the trams as of a peculiar shape not like a railway wagon or ordinary road cart. The early ones were almost certainly constructed of wood with cast iron wheels although in later

years all-iron designs may have been introduced. Most trams probably had some form of hand brake but no definite details seem to be
known.

Toll permits from the 1820s show that the larger trams could hold
as much as 2 tons 18 cwt of stone. Assuming a tare weight of 15 cwt
this totals 3 tons 13 cwt, or 17 cwt in excess of the permitted
maximum. No wonder the tramplates broke! Because the narrow
gauge cramped the body width, capacity was probably made up in
length, although another method would have been to extend the
upper part of the body over the wheels.

It is interesting to compare conditions on the Hay Railway, where
an identical permanent way was employed. Here, the laden weight
was limited to 50 cwt.

The trams were probably linked together by short chains or
shackles, and in some instances, if not all, the horse worked between
shafts, as with a road wagon. The shafts were fixed to the front tram
by a transverse pin and the breakage of one on a coal tram in September 1848 precipitated the driver into its path, with fatal consequences. According to the *Cheltenham Examiner*,

> Deceased was in the employ of Mr Jordan, coal merchant . . . He had been
> repeatedly warned by his master not to ride on the shafts on pain of
> dismissal from his service; but in spite of these warnings he persisted in
> this common but dangerous practice . . .

Obviously the tramroad company had learned to turn a blind eye to
their relevant byelaw and the employers were fairing no better — the
temptation to ride was surely irresistible.

The Devils Chimney

Henry Lamb's drawing of the Devil's Chimney and incline, about 1830.

The tramroad crossing Barton Street, Gloucester, at the tollgates looking towards the docks, *c.*1835.   *Gloucester City Libraries*

The tramroad at Barton Street gates; a view in the opposite direction to the previous illustration.   *Alan Smith*

Four tramplates of three different patterns. The top two with curved ends are from the main line and the others come from Leckhampton.   *David Bick*

A fruitful dig aided by an ex-W.D. mine detector, 1966. The low ridge marking the route beyond Longlevens has since been ploughed out.

David Bick

Chapter Five
Operation and Commerce

Early railways were often known as "railroads". They were quite logically looked upon as an improved form of road where easily graded rails enabled far heavier loads to be moved. Provided the rules and regulations of the company were obeyed, anyone could put a horse and tram upon the line, and the principle of erecting toll houses and extracting payment from the users was practised in just the same manner as on turnpike roads. Hence the term "railroad" aptly described the new mode of transport, and it is worth recalling that to this day railwaymen speak of the permanent way as "the road".

In January 1812 the company issued its Bye Laws, Order and Regulations, "For the Government and Good Order of the Railway", over the name of its agent, William Tillard. They amounted to twenty-four items to be inwardly digested by users, with penalties for non-compliance. Here are three examples.

1. "That if a waggon shall by accident get off the plates, the driver shall immediately use every effort to replace it, and if it shall have been dragged out of its track more than ten yards, he shall for every yard it shall have been so dragged, over and above ten, forfeit and pay the sum of Five Shillings."
2. "That any driver of a waggon who shall have a tram-nail in an axle-tree instead of a proper linch-pin, shall for each offence, forfeit and pay the sum of Twenty Shillings."
3. "That when loaded waggons are travelling in opposite directions the driver of the gang which shall not have passed the distance-post placed midway between each passing-place and marked D, shall immediately draw back to the passing-place behind him and remain there until the others have gone forward.

   "That when empty and loaded wagons meet between two passing-places the driver of the empty ones shall in all cases immediately draw back to the passing-place behind him. And any waggoner offending shall for each offence forfeit and pay any sum not exceeding Five Pounds nor less than Ten Shillings."

This latter rule was clearly very open to interpretation depending on the state of loading; probably the more forceful drivers paid little heed to it. There were of course neither signals nor timetable to regulate the traffic, except at Tramway Crossing where a semaphore is said to have been installed.

A few years later the Hay Tramroad in Breconshire, also a 3 ft 6 in. gauge plateway, issued almost identical Regulations, and it would be interesting to trace the original source of these primitive railway rule books.

Railway tolls were on a more advanced basis than turnpike tolls,

Benjamin Newmarch's bill to Sheldon & Haines for tolls for stone, weighing, and rent of wharf.
G.R.O.

the rates depending on the cargo weight and to a lesser extent on its value. The maximum values of these rates were laid down by the authorizing Act, but lower ones were sometimes set to attract trade.

The tramroad company announced the following rates in June 1812 for the full distance from Gloucester to Cheltenham; rates were proportionally rather higher for shorter journeys.

Description of Goods	Rate per Ton	s.	d.
Manure, Stone for repair of Roads	... ...		8½
Coal or Coke ...		2	0
Stone (except Road Stone) Gravel, Clay, Sand, Lime, Brick, Slate, Timber, Iron or other metal, Pot or Pearl-ash, Hay, Straw, un-threashed Corn, Potatoes, brewers Grains, or like articles ...		2	1
Beer, Ale, or Porter, in Cask	... ...	2	6
Threashed Corn, Flour, Malt, Hops, Cheese, Groceries, manu factured Goods, Goods in Package, and other than as above		3	0

Four weighing machines were installed and were situated at Gloucester docks, the Cheltenham depot, Leckhampton Junction and at the end of the branch by the foot of the inclines to Trye's quarries. Later, a fifth machine was added at the company's Gloucester depot in Park Road. There is, however, some evidence to suggest that the Leckhampton Junction machine had gone out of use before 1838.

By the company's regulations, trams had to carry their owner's names in large white letters, together with the registered number, and the unladen weight was to be displayed on both sides. At the toll office housing the weighing machine, the driver received a permit signed by the toll clerk giving the registered numbers of his trams, their net weight and other details. Two formats were current in the 1820s, one for the main line and one for the branch. The column headed "Owner" referred to the owner of the goods rather than the tram itself, although quite often the two were synonymous.

The tramroad company, finding trade slow to start, advertised in March 1813 for "any person to establish himself as a common carrier on the Railway". He was to be given a lock-up warehouse rent free,and reduced toll rates for groceries and light articles was a further inducement.

Wharves and warehouses were let to traders at the Cheltenham depot, but at the other end of the line, both traders and the company rented these facilities from the Gloucester and Berkeley Canal, the necessary sidings usually being laid by the tenants. One wharf at the docks was reserved for public use.

About 1824 the overcrowded dock area was relieved by the provision of a small basin, the "Barge Arm", complete with wharves and yards to which no less than eighteen sidings were extended. The

Gloucester and Cheltenham Railway.

PERMIT, No. *67* from LECKHAMPTON HILL

to *Mr Jessop*

PLACE OF DEPOSIT.	DESCRIPTION OF LADING.	NUMBER OF WAGGONS.	WEIGHT.			AT PER TON.	AMOUNT.		
			TONS.	CWT.	QRS.		£	s.	d.
Grotten's Wharf	*Rough Gravel*	*33*	*1*	*8*					
		TOTAL	*1*	*8*					

Dated this *16th* Day of *Sept* *E J Wills* 18*35* Toll Clerk.

[Please to keep this Permit to prevent mistakes.]

Griffith and Co. Chronicle Office.

Gloucester and Cheltenham Railway.

PERMIT No. *3390* from *Glo* to *Chel*

Owner.	Driver.	Description of Lading.	Number of Waggons.	Weight.			Miles Rate	Amount.		
				Tons	Cwt.	Qrs.		£	s.	d.
Mr Maule	*John Hale*	*Bristol Stone*		*2*	*5*					
				2	*3*	*2*				
				2	*5*					
				2	*2*	*2*				
				2	*3*					

Dated this *4* Day of *April* 18*29*

Toll-Clerk.

Lamfdn

Johnson, Printer and Engraver, Cheltenham.

Toll Permits. *Top:* Rough gravel from Leckhampton to Grotten's Wharf.
Bottom: Bristol stone from Gloucester to Cheltenham for the town surveyor,
Mr Maule. *GRO*

tramroad company seems to have sublet some of its wharves at the new basin and traded over the line on its own account. In November 1838, Henry Lucy rather saucily tried to get a drawback from the Gloucester and Berkeley on wharfage charged for coal landed beyond his company's premises, but was unlucky.

When need arose, wharves were also established at various points on the line, and land owners, through whose ground the route passed, were permitted by the 1809 Act to make sidings or branches at their own expense. One such siding at Westall Green on the Leckhampton branch nearly landed certain gentlemen in trouble in October 1825.

> . . . Pearson Thompson Esquire, Edward Armitage Esquire and Mr. William Clapham have encroached on Westal Green (part of the Waste Lands within this Manor) by having placed and left large quantities of Timber, Bricks, Stone, Coal and other Materials thereon, by which the public Road leading across the same is greatly impeded and also by having destroyed the surface of part of the said Green and converted the same into a Rail-Road for their own private purposes . . .

They were ordered to remove the line and materials and make good the damage within ten days. Many similar sidings came and went, of which no record remains. Between Cheltenham and Gloucester a wharf was located near Arle Court where Badgeworth Lane joins the main road. There were probably others at Staverton Bridge and Longlevens.

Most coal and other traders regularly using the line had their own drivers, trams and horses, but in the 1830s the Cheltenham Town Commissioners hired trams from a Mr Thomas White at 9d. each per day and the drivers worked on contract, providing horses into the bargain.

As a rule, two laden trams were about the maximum for one horse, the limit being imposed by the climb from Staverton Bridge. Near here, close by the Plough Inn, the tramroad company possessed a long low stone building. It was reputedly to stable horses, their purpose doubtless being to help the heavier loads to the summit. At Arle Court, where the gradient steepened to 1 in 100, a horse was also available and a pathway descending from the line to the Hatherley Brook was probably constructed for the convenience of watering the animal.

A train of roadstone for the Commissioners usually comprised two or four trams holding rather over two tons apiece, although on 26th March, 1829, six trams brought up 14 tons. This was exceeded on 17th December, 1829 by a load of 16 tons 13 cwt 2 qtrs, for which the gross weight would have been about 21 tons. These heavy trains with their straining horses and clattering trams must have presented a fine sight.

The round trip of 17 miles to Gloucester and back constituted a typical day's work, involving six or seven hours on the move. Allowing for loading and unloading and time waiting in passing loops (laden trams had preference over empties), the whole day was accounted for and any spare time could be agreeably spent in one or more of the sixteen pubs lining the route.

The Waggoners' Arms beerhouse, now the Golden Valley Café, was a favourite haunt of the drivers, some of whom on 7th November, 1840 tarried too long, their trams meanwhile blocking the line. This led to Henry Lucy bringing a summons against the landlord, Isaac Withers, but the case was adjourned until an unfortunate lad whose hand had been severed by a tram was well enough to give evidence! Withers was frequently before the bench for offences involving drunkenness and serving after hours, and once for a paternity case.

Children, of course, found a tram ride irresistible. Adults were also carried in a rough and ready way, no doubt sometimes in exchange for a trifle given to the driver, and in 1831 the *Cheltenham Journal* was complaining about the influx of tramps and vagrants arriving over the line. This unofficial service was largely responsible for many tragic accidents, the first being in August 1812 when

> . . . a boy belonging to a poor woman who has seven small children . . . by some accident fell whilst travelling on the Railroad, and a tram wheel passing over him, fractured his knee joint, and leg in such a dreadful manner, that amputation of the thigh was found necessary to preserve the sufferer's life . . .

Two further incidents occurred in October 1827.

> . . . a little boy named Samuel Poulton was riding on a railway tram loaded with coal, one of the large pieces was shook off, which fell upon his thigh and fractured it . . .

> . . . Thomas Fletcher, a little boy about seven years of age, was left to take care of five trams on the railway road, when endeavouring to stop the horses, he by some means got underneath and they went over him . . .

A holiday trip to Barton Fair at Gloucester, led to tragedy in October 1840.

> . . . a lad named Lea, . . . obtained leave to go to Barton fair with a companion; seeing several trams they asked if they might be allowed to ride, and without waiting for an answer, Lea's companion jumped into one of the trams. Lea attempted to follow him, but missing his step fell under the wheel and was killed on the spot.

Haulage over the tramroad, although cheaper than by road, was expensive compared with conveyance by water. In the 1830s road-stone from James Poole's Blackrock Quarry in the Avon Gorge, Bristol, was being shipped and delivered to Gloucester at the remarkably low price of 4/1d. per ton; by 1848 the price had actually fallen to 4/- per ton, including 6d. canal dues, wharf rent and loading the trams.

Cost of carriage per ton by tramroad to Cheltenham was compounded as follows:

								s.	d.
Tram hire	...	...	...	...	...	...	...		4
Horse and driver	...	...	...	...	...	...	...	2	0
Toll charges	...	...	...	...	...	...	...		8½
								3	0½

These charges were enough to render the alternative and longer route via the Coombe Hill Canal not altogether uncompetitive and in 1829, if not later, small amounts of stone were reaching the town in this way.

Regarding traffic from Cheltenham to Gloucester little has come to light. By an agreement with the tramroad company, Trye's stone from Leckhampton went toll-free over the main line, which no doubt explains the omission of this important item in the tramroad accounts for 1838 (see later). In the early years large quantities of pipes were conveyed from the Guiting stone pipe works, but this business unfortunately soon collapsed, as is explained in Chapter 8.

As an indication of the traffic generated during Cheltenham's building boom, in the period 1831–6 one builder alone (R.W. Gerrard) conveyed no less than 11,725 tons of coal, timber, slate and other materials over the line from Gloucester.

With regard to coal traffic, to increase their trade the Worcester and Birmingham Canal Company had leased the Coombe Hill Canal and by the mid 1830s half of Cheltenham's coal was being dragged by road from the tiny basin at Coombe Hill. Almost all of the remainder, of course, came from the Forest of Dean via the tramroad, but the total cost of carriage was considerable, and, in spite of the tramroad company cutting tolls to 1/9d., coal tonnages stayed virtually constant.

In an effort to reduce the cost of Forest coal, various influential Cheltenham residents proposed a new line, the Gloucester and Dean Forest Railway, to avoid the old route via the Bullo Pill Tramroad, the Severn, and the Gloucester and Cheltenham Tramroad. In evidence they produced some illuminating facts relating to transport costs in 1844.

	s.	d.
Price at Pit's Mouth	7	0
Tonnage and Wharfage to Bullo Pill	1	9
Hauling and Tram	1	9
Shipping at Bullo Pill		4
Freight to Gloucester	2	0
Lockage at Gloucester		3
Hauling on to Cheltenham	2	0
Tonnage on Tramroad	1	6
Wharfage at Cheltenham		4
	16	2

It will be noted that, by this time, rates for coal on the tramroad had fallen to 1/6d., a figure which seems to have applied for the remainder of its days.

One of the very few official documents of the tramroad company known to have survived, is the "Statement of the gross Tonnages, Receipts and Expenses, and net Revenue of the Gloucester and Cheltenham Tram Road for the Year 1838". This solitary sheet, signed by Henry Lucy, reveals much about the economics of the line during its best years, and allows some interesting deductions to be made.

TRAMROAD ACCOUNTS, 1838

Coals at 1/9	Road Stone at 8½d.	Sundries	Total	Leckhampton Tramroad	Amount
Tons Cwt.	Tons Cwt.	Tons Cwt.	Tons Cwt.	Tons Cwt.	£ s. d.
26,215 7	6,897 16	2,762 8	35,875 11	22,938 4	2,916 13 9½

Total Produce				Total Expenses			
	£ s. d.				£ s. d.		
Tonnages	2,916 13 9½		Printing	39 3 6			
Wharfages	32 17 5½		Salaries	215 0 0			
Rents	242 2 6		Annual Payments ...	52 3 1			
Weighbridge	68 4 4		Wages	241 14 7			
Tram Hire	232 11 1½		Rates and Taxes ...	91 5 6			
Metal sold	56 16 1½		Incidents	44 19 0			
			Tram Plates ...	159 7 11½			
			Repair to Buildings	72 3 9			
			Repair to Trams ...	151 9 1			
			Block Gravelling ...	69 14 5			
			Law Expenses ...	25 19 9			
			Bad Debts	79 7 9½			
			Deduct of last year's	1,242 7 8			
			Expenses	72 10 0			
				1,169 17 8			
			Net Revenue	2,379 7 8			
	£3,549 5 4			£3,549 5 4			

(Signed) H. LUCY JANUARY 1839

Coal provided easily the greatest source of revenue, followed by sundries and roadstone. The weighbridge, which contributed £68 4s. 4d., was installed outside the Cheltenham depot in 1813 for road vehicles, charges being 3d. per cart and 6d. per wagon. Income derived from tram hire was largely swallowed by repairs, and must have rendered the business hardly worthwhile. "Metal sold" refers to broken tramplates for scrap and the replacement cost (£159 7s. 11½d.) gives an idea of the annual number of breakages, which works out at 975 (one fortieth of the whole route) assuming new plates cost £8 per ton. Theft of plates was another common expense, and one James Capper got a comparatively light sentence of 12 months' hard labour in March 1837 for removing no less than 58.

The expenditure on salaries and wages suggests that the tramroad employed about ten people in all, if we assume £2 per week for Lucy, £1 for the toll clerks and ten shillings for the platelayers, labourers, etc.

The tramroad's prosperity fluctuated considerably over its fifty year span. In 1812, a year after the line opened, £100 shares were fetching £80, but by 10th May, 1815, the company was £8,188 19s. 4d. in debt and had still not entirely completed the works. The money-raising Act of 1815 resolved these problems, but share values fell heavily and a year later Lord Sherborne bought 18¾ shares at only £35 each. In spite of the extra capital, shares were still quoted in terms of the original authorized capital of £35,000 (350 at £100 par), and on this basis *The Financial and Commercial Record* quoted as follows:

Date	Half yearly Dividend	Price
October 1819	£4	£80
March 1821	£4	£80
July 1823	Not quoted	£40
April 1824	Not quoted	£40
November 1824	£4	£80
June 1825	Not quoted	£78
July 1828	Not quoted	£78

As previously mentioned, there was no dividend in 1829 but the company seems soon to have regained its old form and by 1838 profits were £2,379 7s. 8d., amounting to 6.8% dividend.

According to Birmingham & Gloucester and Midland Railway records, profits after 1840 were as follows.

Year	Profits	Year	Profits
1841	£2,100	1851	£925
1842	£1,925	1852	£350*
1843	£1,750	1853	Not quoted

Year	Profits	Year	Profits
1844	£1,750	1854	£345*
1845	Not quoted	1855	£123
1846	Not quoted	1856	£178
1847	Not quoted	1857	£138
1848	Not quoted	1858	£54*
1849	£700*	1859	Not quoted
1850	£1,050	1860	Not quoted

* Half year.

The rapid fall after 1849 reflects competition arising from the Midland Railway's arrival at the High Orchard docks. After 1854, the further decline can be attributed to the results of direct rail access from the Forest of Dean to Cheltenham.

Chapter Six

Steam on the Line

The repeated efforts to introduce steam traction on the Gloucester and Cheltenham Tramroad are one of its most absorbing aspects. The possibilities were being considered only ten years after the line opened, and locomotives were actually tried in 1825 and again six or seven years later, all this preceding the firm establishment of modern railways.

To add perspective before going into detail, a little should be said about the general background to locomotive development to the end of this period.

The world's first locomotive was completed in 1804 by Richard Trevithick for the Pen y Darren Tramroad (a plateway similar to the Gloucester and Cheltenham) from Merthyr Tydfil to Abercynon. Although only a partial success, the trials marked a great technical advance, for hitherto steam power had been associated almost exclusively with machinery far too ponderous and bulky for mobile applications.

After Trevithick left the scene, many striving inventors put forward in all seriousness some very daring and unusual designs, often to be taken up by credulous parties whose enthusiasm clouded their judgement. But in one important respect the course of progress to a great extent followed different lines, so to speak, from those pioneered by Trevithick. In general, horse tramroad permanent way could barely stand the passage of normal traffic, let alone the greater loadings of steam locomotives. Although, in spite of this limitation, a few tramroads did apply steam, the real advances took place in locomotives designed for edge railways, in the north of England where significantly the plateway was virtually unknown.

These advances inhibited and finally stopped developments of tramroads and tramroad locomotives. Even so, by the 1830s various such engines were in use on South Wales tramroads, in some cases lasting long enough to be eventually converted for standard gauge purposes. Speeds and axle loadings, however, were very restricted and such applications provided the exception proving the rule that tramroads and locomotives formed an uneasy alliance.

Encouraged by progress on edge railways, at an early stage, a few farsighted men foresaw the whole country linked with steam lines. One was William James, a solicitor and land-agent of Henley-in-Arden, Warwickshire. He visited George Stephenson at Killingworth, Northumberland, in the summer of 1821 to become better acquainted with the powers of the new form of locomotion.

We now return to the Gloucester and Cheltenham Tramroad, for a few months later James was in Gloucester writing to Stephenson for advice about an engine for the line. Stephenson's reply was cautious.

TO: Wm. James Esqre.,
    West Bromwich,
        Nr. Birmingham.

My dear Sir,
    . . . Before I could advise the use of an Engine on the Cheltenham Railroad, you must give me the weight of the Rail p. yd.—whether the Line descends with or without the loaded waggons also inside breadth of the Railroad, weight of waggons and goods working on the said Line whether the Line is uniform in descent from end to end. We have no Engines to spare in case the above Railroad should be found suitable for them. We are expecting to commence making 3 Locomotive Engines in a fortnight's time for a neighbouring Colliery. If the Cheltenham way was found suitable we might commence making one for you at the same time but I am afraid it will not. I should be unwilling to recommend an Engine on any Line unless I was confident of it giving satisfaction . . .

> I am Dear Sir
> Yours sincerely,
> (Signed) G. Stephenson.

Killingworth Colls.
Oct. 7th 1821.

The letter implies that James had connections with the tramroad company, but in any event it seems unlikely that the matter proceeded beyond this enquiry.

The next reference to steam on the line comes in 1825 when Benjamin Newmarch, already a man of many parts, was involved with a locomotive of novel concept. The *Cheltenham Journal* for 17th January, under the heading "NEW STEAM CARRIAGE", made this announcement.

A loco-motive engine, upon an entirely new principle, will be exhibited, in the course of a few days, on the Cheltenham and Gloucester Rail Road, and it is intended to ply regularly between that City and the coal wharf of Mr. B. Newmarch, by whom the experiment will be made with the first carriage that has yet started upon the same construction, as it is formed without a boiler, and consequently without the slightest risk of explosion.

It appears the engine was based on a patent taken out in 1824 (No. 4974) by Major John McCurdy of Cecil Street, London, for a form of flash boiler. According to Galloway, writing in 1830, "this invention originated in America where great anticipations were entertained, and it was announced in the public journals of England and Europe not merely as an important discovery in science, but as forming almost an era in the history of the steam engine. Mr McCurdy

The bronze ticket issued for the ill-fated passenger service on the Gloucester & Cheltenham Tramroad, 1831/2. *David Bick*

brought the invention over to this country and sold his patent right for a large sum."

The boiler consisted of a thick-walled cylinder like a gun-barrel, 11 ft long and tapering from one end to the other. Water from a pump was forced through a mesh of radial drillings within a tube protruding concentrically into the large end. The whole was immersed in a firebox, the water being flashed into steam on contacting the red-hot inner surface of the cylinder.

That at least was the theory, and we can understand how the concept, so simple and cheap to execute, found many supporters. In the history of engineering the time had not come when detailed appraisal followed by tests automatically preceded the final product, or fiascos like the Stone Pipe Co. (Chapter 2) would not have occurred. Such an approach might have been interpreted as a grave lack of confidence on the part of the inventor. At all events, these trials on the Gloucester & Cheltenham tramroad were taken seriously enough to anticipate the presence "of all the practical engineers in the country."

Delays unfortunately resulted, but a few months later the *Cheltenham Chronicle* announced a further attempt on 12th May, 1825. "The necessary arrangements having been completed, we understand that the locomotive will start this day from Mr Newmarch's wharf in Gloucester and arrive in this town about 2 o'clock . . . We heartily wish all possible success to this spirited undertaking." But nothing further was heard. Neither has anything come to light as to the makers or financial backers, though we can strongly suspect that Newmarch, with his fingers in so many industrial pies including coal works in the Forest of Dean, was closely involved.

The reasons behind the failure were the quite inadequate surface area of the boiler, and the almost impossible task of matching the feed-water to the varying demands of the engine. There is, however, an interesting item in the *Register of Arts & Sciences* 5th February, 1825, which states that a carriage on McCurdy's principle was under construction for use on ordinary roads. As long ago as 1901 *The Engineer* went to much trouble to ascertain the outcome of these trials but without success.

The McCurdy episode had not long passed when proposals came about for a railway from Bath to Bristol using locomotive engines, a matter which the *Cheltenham Journal* reported on 16th November, 1829. The paper was obviously unaware of the tramroad company's temporary financial plight and concluded. . .

> We would submit to the Proprietors of the tramroad line to Gloucester whether it would not be in their interest and the public convenience to

substitute a rail road in lieu of tramplates, and adopt the plan of locomotive engines for conveying passengers and goods, as we think the
superiority of a rail, and the advantage of carrying passengers would soon
remunerate them for the extra cost . . .

Rather more than a year later, in February 1831, Sir Charles Dance
put one of Goldsworthy Gurney's steam coaches on the Gloucester–
Cheltenham turnpike road and several thousand passengers were
carried before opposition brought the experiment to an end.

In 1830 one of Gurney's engines, suitably modified, had been tried
on William Crawshay's tramroad at Hirwain in South Wales, and
another followed in 1831. These developments on road and rail
would not have gone unnoticed, and very shortly afterwards the
Gloucester & Cheltenham Railway Co. acquired its own locomotive,
the *Royal William*.

We may presume that the vision of passenger traffic was the major
incentive. Dance had shown what steam could do, and demonstrated
the demand; there were in fact at this period no less than 80 coaches
every week running between the town and city. The deficiencies of a
plateway for anything resembling speed were clearly not thought
serious, and as for the problem of operating steam on a line choked
with slow horse-traffic, had this not been resolved on the tramroads
of South Wales? Twenty sets of wheels and axles were ordered in
addition to the *Royal William*, and their light-weight design leaves
little doubt as to the purpose.

There is also the testimony of bronze medals, two of which are in
Cheltenham's Museum and now very rare items (see illustration).
Early railway tickets were of this kind, being handed in at the end of
the journey for re-issue. Two types were struck for the Gloucester &
Cheltenham Tramroad, *Class No. 1* and *Class No. 2*. The former presumably corresponded to carriages having the special wheels noted
above, whilst Class No. 2 holders rode in ordinary tram-wagons.

The *Royal William* duly arrived in Gloucester, probably in a coaster,
and was tried out at a date never quite established, for the press,
mindful of earlier debacles, reported nothing. However, it was very
likely the winter of 1831/2.

The engine came from the Neath Abbey ironworks near Swansea,
and a little about the early locomotives of this firm will not be amiss.
Founded in 1792, the Neath Abbey ironworks turned out a variety of
engineering products and in 1829 started manufacturing tramroad
locomotives of widely varying design, some displaying great orig-
inality. Many drawings of the detail parts and assemblies of these
engines have been preserved at the Glamorgan Record Office, Cardiff
where they may now be seen in restored condition. Although some

The *Royal William*, built at Neath Abbey Ironworks in 1831, reconstructed as far as can be confidently predicted from existing drawings.

Wheel Arrangement	0–6–0
Wheel diameter	3 ft 9in.
Wheelbase	3 ft 10½in. x 3 ft 10½in.
Track of Wheels	3 ft 9in.
Cylinder Position	Vertical
Cylinder dimension	10½in. x 20in. stroke
Boiler diameter	3 ft 10in.
Boiler length	12 ft
Tractive effort at 50 lb/in. boiler pressure	2,440 lb at 100% pressure

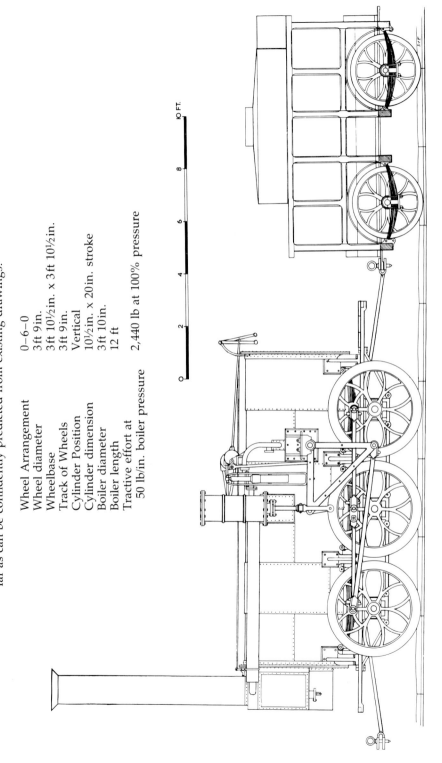

Note: The actual working pressure is uncertain, but was probably the same as *Camel* — 50 lb/in².

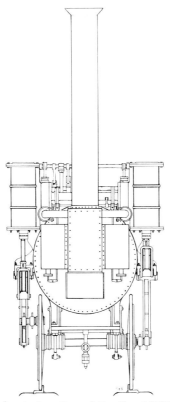

The front elevation of the *Royal William.*

are missing and others marked with neither date nor title, in several cases it is possible to largely reconstruct the appearance of the engines, and to understand the relationship of one with another.

Most of the early engines including a rack locomotive had an 0–6–0 wheel arrangement. They were characterized by a strong family likeness, the only exception being the disposition of the cylinders, about which Neath Abbey could never make up its mind. Though the vertical cylinder and bell-crank arrangement proved favourite, inclined cylinders facing either back or forth on the side of the boiler or even horizontally located high up and driving via rocking-levers were all tried. There must have been good reason for these variations, for cylinders between the frames had been contemplated, if not actually used, for a 2 ft 9 in. gauge 0–4–0 plateway engine in 1831.

Of the first 0–6–0 bell-crank engines, one named *Hercules* was for Prothero, another for Harford Bros of Ebbw Vale, and a third for the Gloucester & Cheltenham Tramroad — the *Royal William*. Others were the *Lark*, and the *Camel* and *Elephant* for the Bodmin and Wadebridge Railway.

These six-coupled bell-crank locomotives may be summarised as follows:

Date	Name	Customer	Cylinders	Gauge
1830	*Hercules*	Prothero	10½ x 24″	4′2″ plateway
1830	—	Harford	10½ x 24″	4′2″ plateway
1831	*R. William*	G&C Rly Co.	10½ x 20″	3′6″ plateway
c.1832	*Lark*	Harford, Davies		4′2″ plateway
1834	*Camel*	Bodmin &	10½ x 24″	4′8½″ Edge rail
1836	*Elephant*	Wadebridge	12 x 24″	

The *Camel*, as used on the Bodmin & Wadebridge line.

Making allowance for its smaller size, an idea of the cost and weight of the *Royal William* can be gained from the *Camel* which was 12½ tons full, and 725 tons complete with tender. In its best years the Gloucester & Cheltenham Tramroad could have paid such a sum out of profits within a few months.

If somewhat lagging behind the best practice of the day, Neath

Abbey locomotives were soundly built and endured years of punishment on the rough plateways of South Wales. A graphic description of a ride behind *Perseverance* has been quoted in *Steam on the Penydarren* by M.J.T. Lewis.

Turning now to the *Royal William* in detail, the design was in certain respects unusual, not to say freakish, as if the makers had taken the liberty of trying out their latest notions at the customer's expense. Surviving drawings fall between June and November 1831, although one "boiler with additional tubes" is dated 31st December, 1831. Whether this implies an afterthought, a last minute modification, or an alteration following an unsatisfactory trial is not known.

The drawings make it clear that the boiler departed from standard practice, being of the water-tube variety. The overall length was 12 ft, with a corrugated crown to the firebox, the latter measuring about 4 ft 6 in. long and 3 ft wide. A very large flue conveyed the hot gases to the smokebox and contained 45 vertical water-tubes about 2½ in. diameter and 21 in. long. These were not spread uniformly, but fore and aft in a narrow row, allowing much heat to pass by. Also, a very low gas velocity would have rendered the boiler a poor steamer, which probably explains the additional tubes.

The flue ended in a complicated smokebox housing a free-running 16 in. diameter fan of no apparent purpose. There were also two large valves, perhaps for regulating the draught and operating by a long rod from the footplate. The funnel or stack rose 15 ft above the track, or 18 in. higher than the maximum on modern railways.

The cylinders measured 10½ x 20 in., with the slide-valves facing inwards. These were not worked from the motion or from eccentrics on the axles, but by a counter-shaft running across the boiler and rotated by cranks and connecting-rods from the bell-cranks. Two eccentrics joined at 90° but loose on the shaft could be driven from either end by one or other dog-clutches set 180° apart. The reversing lever determined which clutch engaged. Each eccentric was also connected to a hand-lever at the footplate and both levers oscillated continuously with the engine in motion. The cut-off could not be varied.

To start, the driver juggled the eccentrics and reversing lever into the desired mesh, this being equivalent to full forward gear. To stop, the engine was put into reverse; there were no brakes. To hold the train on an incline it appears that spragging the wheels was the only way.

In addition to the boiler, feed-water heating presented another peculiarity. It appears from the drawings that instead of jacketing the feed-pipe between pump and boiler with exhaust steam, the Neath

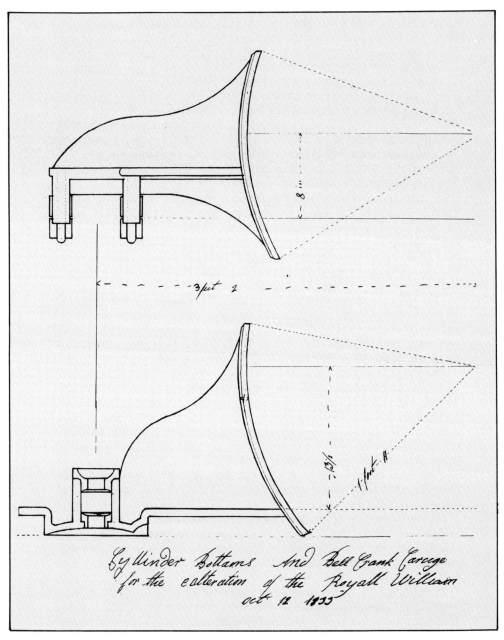

Neath Abbey drawings of new mountings for the *Royal William's* bell-cranks and cylinders, for conversion to a wider gauge.   *Gwent R.O.*

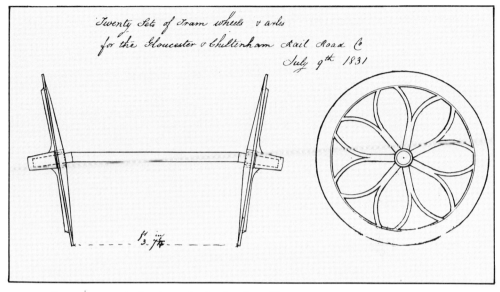

Twenty sets of Tram wheels & axles for the Gloucester & Cheltenham Rail Road Co. July 9th 1831

Twenty sets of wheels and axles for the "Gloucester & Cheltenham Rail Road Co.", 9th July, 1831.
Gwent R.O.

Abbey company chose for the *Royal William* a very unusual, not to say unique alternative. According to the drawings the feed-water was heated on the suction or inlet side of the pump. Whatever advantage may have resulted, on the debit side the latter then had to cope with hot or even boiling water with the attendant problems of corrosion and cavitation. This feature may partly explain the observations at the trials, as will be described shortly.

The remaining curiosity about the *Royal William* was its enclosure in a wooden box which descended to within a foot of the ground. The locomotive historian Dendy Marshall took it to be a packing-case for transporting the engine, but more probably it served to prevent scaring horses in busy streets. The case is illustrated in his *A History of Railway Locomotives down to the end of the Year 1831*.

For evidence of the trials we are indebted to a local antiquarian, the late H.Y.J. Taylor, who interviewed two elderly witnesses and wrote an account to the *Gloucestershire Echo*. His letters published 24th December, 1896 and 22nd March, 1897 are worth quoting almost in entirety. The first also contains interesting details not included here, about Sir Charles Dance's steam coach service on the Gloucester and Cheltenham road in 1831.

The Old Cheltenham and Gloucester Railway
To the Editor of the "Echo"

Sir,

I had a visit from Thomas Phelps who has reached his 84th birthday. I asked him if he remembered the old Cheltenham and Gloucester tramway which commenced at Gloucester Quay, and extended to the bottom of High Street, Cheltenham. He said his recollection of it was very vivid. I asked him if he remembered when an abortive attempt was made to run a locomotive engine from Gloucester to Cheltenham. He said he did. I understood that only one tentative trip was made, but he said that more than one attempt was made, and the startling adventure was hopelessly abandoned. He said the tramway metals were laid on stones, or stone blocks, and the engine was frequently off, and had to be heaved on again.

"I (said Thomas Phelps) ran alongside on him—sometimes he was on and sometimes he was off. We started from the coal yard . . . It took some time to make the water bile to get the steam up and to get un to move. He did at last and he ran along till the metals kicked up and the engine was off. It was hard work to get un to Barnwood but he spinned away at a good speed from Barnwood pike to opposite the Turnpike on the Cheltenham Road. It was as much as I could kip up with un that distance. There he stuck and he would not budge one inch furder. They had a terrible bother to get un back home again. Coal was getting short and hardly water enough inside on him to bile. The Cheltenham people was a looken out for un at the t'other end but he never got to Cheltenham and the Cheltenham folks went home disappointed saying 'twas all humbug. They made a last trial and crowds of Gloucester people went to see the show. They was sartin sure he would run to Cheltenham and would be there in an hour or so. The Cheltenham folks again went out to meet un. They let the fire in him, filled his belly full of water, puffed at the fire with a bellows, and made him bile and bubble. They brought un out of the coal yard a boiling and a bubbling, a roaring, a blazing, and a blowing off clouds of smoke and ashes; he coughed, groaned, grunted and snorted; by and bye he began to run and we run arter un. Before he got to Barton pike he kicked and scouted on the metals, he groaned, he squealed and grunted, the fire rushed out, the sparks fled out and the steam and smoke rolled above in clouds and in a moment a terrible noise was yurd. We all fled back. We soon found out what was the matter. The blessed thing had busted. The driver got off just in time or he would have been roasted to cinders or biled or scalded to death. No: he never lived to reach Cheltenham. We thought that would be the end of these steam wunderments. Wot wut them old foggies say too't now? Twud open their peepers to see the old Flying Scotchman galloping along like lightning horse at the reet of 60 miles a minut. Some people said this engine would be the making of Cheltenham, some said 'twud be the ruin on't 'cause the noise and smoke would frighten the gentry out o' the pleece. But they could never get the varment to go so fur. They could neither coax nor force un to go beyond the Cheltenham pike . . ."

Taylor's second letter, with its delightful title, is as follows:

The Old Engine of the Original Cheltenham and Gloucester Railway
To the Editor of the "Echo"

Sir,

Today I had a visit from an aged man, John Godfrey Maliphant . . . I asked Maliphant if he remembered the engine. He said he did very well. It was put on the Gloucester and Cheltenham [tram] road but the difficulties were so many and so great that the efforts to run it did not last longer than a week. . . .

Maliphant said the metals on the tramway were narrow and not very long and were fixed with rough rivets on stones. As the engine pursued its heavy course, the metals tipped up and the men followed behind to replace them. Of course, as you know, the whole thing busted. If the metals had been right, the engine would have done its work right enough. I said, "What became of the engine after the busting or failure?" "Why", said Maliphant, "it was put in the Cheltenham and Gloucester or the Gloucester and Cheltenham coalyard, [*Spa Wharf*] . . . and there he remained for some time till it got rusty".

Mr. Church, the father of Mrs. Kedgwen Hoskyns Fryer, had the management of the Tramway and a Mr. Lambert looked after the yard and lived upon the premises. I asked Maliphant to tell me when he saw the engine make the experimental trip. He paused at several mnemonical mental milestones and answered, "68 years ago, and I baint far out!" That would be 1829 . . .

Maliphant was too early with the date, but both men agreed that the permanent way caused the failure. This problem may have been anticipated and possibly the promoters had determined to see if they could get away with it; if not, to convert the line to an edge railway and alter the locomotive to suit. In support of this theory, drawings were actually prepared at Neath Abbey Ironworks in October 1833 "for the alteration of the Royal William" to standard gauge. On the other hand, many private traders owning trams would have objected and the change would have been very costly.

Another tantalizing drawing, but in an entirely different hand, survives in the Neath Abbey collection, and is entitled "Slide Valve box cover and stuffing box for a locomotive for the Gloucester and Cheltenham Railroad Company". It is clearly dated 18th December, 1839. Was this locomotive for the tramroad company ordered in anticipation of heavy traffic between the docks and the new Birmingham & Gloucester station which opened in 1840? At all events, according to Clement Stretton the railway historian, the *Royal William* ended its days on the Birmingham & Gloucester line, as appears from this letter concerning the bronze tickets and published in *Engineering*, 12th March, 1897.

Sir,

The locomotive engine shown upon the ticket was built by George Stephenson for the Duke of Portland in 1817; it was afterwards sold by him to the Gloucester & Cheltenham company and was named 'Royal William'.

It worked the traffic till 1839, when the present railway was constructed upon the ground traversed by the old tramroad. In 1839/40 Mr J.E. McConnell put flanged tyres upon the wheels, but about 1842 the old engine was broken up at the Bromesgrove works . . . I have a diagram of this engine as constructed in 1817. The six wheels were coupled by chains and the engine had steam springs . . .

Clement E. Stretton

With its air of confident authority combined with blatant factual errors, Stretton's account is little more than a joke; nevertheless in regard to the engine's fate it carries a ring of truth and may well be correct.

One fact is definite: the first locomotive ever to reach Cheltenham came by an entirely different route, its presence being reported on 13th July, 1839 by a highly exclusive local newspaper, *The Looker On*.

UNFASHIONABLE ARRIVAL!—On Tuesday last, at noon, the first Locomotive Railway Engine, ever seen in Cheltenham, made its appearance in the High Street, exciting considerable attention as it passed along, drawn by twelve horses, on a carriage apparently prepared for that especial purpose. The lustrous stranger was conveyed along the Promenade and through the new opening near the Queen's Hotel, into the Old Well lane and thence to the railway of the Cheltenham and Great Western Union, at the end of Lansdown Place. This engine has been provided by the contractor, Mr. Oldham, for the purpose of more rapidly and effectually proceeding with the works along theline, upon which it is expected to be in full operation on Monday, commencing its leviathan labours about two miles from the proposed depot. We observed it was very appropriately named *The Excavator* and we have been informed its weight is between eleven and twelve tons.

The engine's appearance must have reminded many Cheltonians of the brave but futile efforts to gain this distinction by means of the tramroad, and some may have wondered, as we wonder now, about the eventual fate of those two old tramroad locomotives, McCurdy's flash boiler engine and the *Royal William*.

Chapter Seven

The Leckhampton Quarries and Tramroads

Leckhampton Hill is one of the most prominent outposts of the Cotswolds, and from its altitude of almost 1000 ft, the views of the Severn Vale and Welsh Border are magnificent. The quarries, described as "moste large" even as early as 1615, have been abandoned for many years, and the area is now best known as a beauty spot and training ground for geologists.

Various materials were exploited during its long industrial history; on the summit, Ragstone beds yielded dry walling stone, roadstone and a highly fossilised stratum prized for garden rockeries. Below, Upper and Lower Freestones, 100 ft in thickness, were removed in large quantities for building and lime burning. The best of the building stone had a fine reputation for durability and purity of colour and was also extensively carved for internal decorations; good examples are to be seen at Magdalen College Chapel, Oxford — one of the most elaborate specimens of the "florid" type, and Cheltenham College Chapel.

At a lower level, gravel was extracted between the 600 and 750 ft contours. The total product output probably exceeded two million tons, nearly all of which came down a complex of tramroads and inclined planes, in use for well over a century.

As the first of these tramroads was possibly the earliest in Gloucestershire, lack of records as to the precise date of introduction is especially regrettable; but the following evidence suggests that it must have quickly followed Charles Brandon Trye's inheritance of the Leckhampton Estate in 1793.

The first quarry exploited by Trye was west of the later workings and a short length of tramroad leading to an incline descending approximately to the 750 ft contour assisted removal of the stone. Construction of the upper part of the incline entailed the excavation of a rock cutting, one side of which was near the escarpment and was afterwards quarried almost entirely away, only a tall pillar of rock remaining. This feature, "The Devil's Chimney" is a famous landmark and the subject of countless picture-postcards. Its origins, having long since been forgotten, have prompted numerous theories which are discussed in my *Old Leckhampton,* but the explanation given here is, I believe, correct.

The Chimney certainly existed before 1803 and we may suppose the tramroads pre-dated it. A Leckhampton antiquarian, the late Alfred Bendall, considered that the incline dates from 1795. As for the edifice itself, after many years of increasing concern its future is now assured, some £20,000 recently having been spent on reinforcing its stability.

71

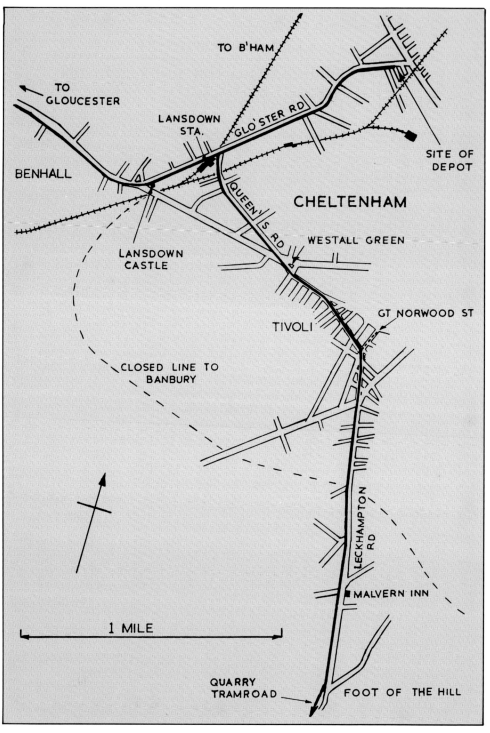

The tramroad including the Leckhampton branch, and the streets which grew around it in Cheltenham.

The 1809 Act empowered the Gloucester and Cheltenham Tram-road to connect its Leckhampton branch to Trye's tramroads on the hill "there already laid down", but a peculiar clause was inserted allowing him to build the last part should the company "neglect, refuse or decline" the task. This clause was probably the consequence of some tacit agreement, for Trye did in due course finance this section which, to quote John Hodgkinson, consisted of "Two incline Planes, including a flat part between, of 950 yds in Length". According to Hodgkinson's estimate, the cost was to be £1,900 including all necessary machinery.

All the hill tramroads and inclines therefore belonged to Trye. The Gloucester and Cheltenham Tramroad's jurisdiction over the Leck-hampton branch ended at the lowest (Bottom) incline, where a weighbridge and two workmen's cottages were soon put up, the latter being demolished about 1950.

The next (Middle) incline rose to the 750 ft contour to a spot which will be termed the "focal point" of later lines on the hill, some 330 yards from the bottom of Devil's Chimney Incline. An interconnect-ing tramroad was probably laid down by April 1810, when the *Cheltenham Chronicle* reported.

The Leckhampton branch at Westall Green in 1830. The new Lansdown Road runs across the line in the middle distance. The area is now a busy road junction and traffic island.   *GRO*

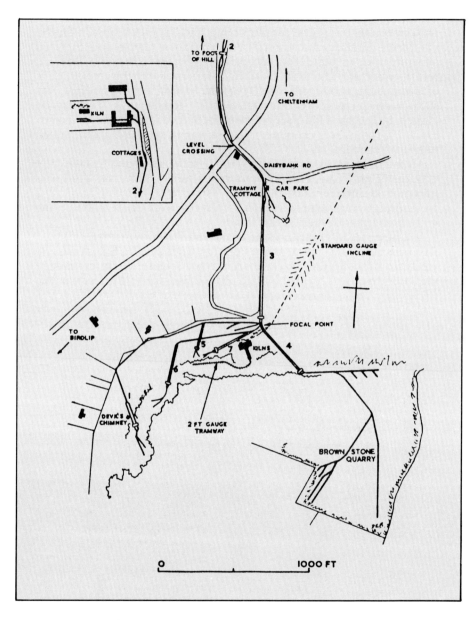

The seven tramroad inclines of Leckhampton Hill.

. . . the inexhaustible stores of Leckhampton Hill are about to be rendered of public utility. A large supply of this stone which is found, on late investigation, to be inferior to none in the island, in point of easiness of conversion, and of durability, has just been contracted for, and the Tram Roads just compleated are already in employ.

Three months later the Leckhampton branch opened and within the next year quarry trams could complete the journey to Gloucester.

Ironically, Trye had little time to enjoy the benefits of these developments. Death removed him, a surgeon and a man greatly respected, on 7th October, 1811.

From the start, Trye's quarries seem to have been worked on a lease, and the tenants had to maintain and extend the tramroad system. Royalties were also charged, depending on the value of the products. The first tenants was John Walford & Co. of Alstone Green — then a hamlet close to Cheltenham. In 1816, Walford was advertising roadstone and gravel at 2s. 3d. per ton, delivered at the bottom of the hill; trade must have been slack, for the announcement ended despairingly — "The Public must be aware that this is cheaper than going to the quarry, if they could be had there for nothing".

The lease was transferred to Benjamin Newmarch in the following year and considerable alterations in the tramroads followed about 1830. Devil's Chimney Incline was abandoned and two very steep replacements appeared. One, No. 5, was 200 yards to the north-east, but later quarrying has long since removed all traces. The other incline, No. 4, was the highest on the hill and rose from the focal point to the summit where the line ran for 200 yds along a shelf to several Ragstone quarries.

By 1829 the lease had passed to George Parker who later took James Vobes as partner. As well as leasing the quarries they also rented part of Grottens Wharf, and during their tenancy, lasting until the 1850s, quarry output approached 30,000 tons per year, later falling with the declining number of new buildings in Cheltenham.

The Leckhampton estate eventually passed to the Rev. (later Canon) C.B. Trye, the younger son of Charles Brandon Trye. In 1859 he was faced with the imminent closure of the Gloucester and Cheltenham Tramroad. Although output was well past its peak, the Leckhampton branch was still the most convenient means of removing the quarry products. Trye opposed the closure, but failed to deter the GWR and the Midland Railway in their proposals. He did, however, manage to gain some sort of compensation. To sugar the pill, the railway companies agreed to sell him, for a nominal ten shillings, the weighbridge and as much of the branch extending over his land at the foot of the hill towards Cheltenham as he required.

The upshot of the concession was that Trye retained about 500 yds of line down the side of Leckhampton Road to a point opposite the Malvern Inn, where he established a stone wharf. This bit of line, the last of the Gloucester and Cheltenham Tramroad, was not taken up until the late 1890s.

After the Leckhampton branch became truncated in 1861, the quarries were worked in a small way by a gentleman named Neighbour Pearman. He was parish clerk of Leckhampton for many years and in 1882 sold 8000 tons of stone and gravel at prices comparable with those of John Walford & Co., 66 years previously. By this time, the building stone trade had died out completely. No tramroads were working west of the focal point but the summit line had been realigned through a shallow cutting towards Hartley Farm for a distance of 350 yards, opening up further Ragstone deposits in the extensive Brownstone Quarry.

In later years, if not from the start, the summit tramroad provided an amenity hardly envisaged by its constructors. By arrangement with Leckhampton traders, groceries and other provisions were carried up in the empty trams to Brownstone Quarry, there to await collection by the villagers of Cowley and Cobberley, some two miles to the south.

A footpath from the villages via the quarry and down beside Middle Incline paved a convenient way to Cheltenham and was regularly used by children walking to school in Leckhampton.

Canon Trye's son, the second Henry Norwood Trye, came into the estate in 1880 and decided to manage the quarries himself, employing Pearman and son as agents. Considerable expansion was planned and four brick-built limekilns and a depot were built on an old brickfield below the workmen's cottages. The depot comprised blacksmiths', wheelwrights' and carpenters' shops, a seven-bay cart shed, stables for eight horses and several rooms for chaff, harness and stores. The horses whose duty was on the hill would make their own way to work each morning. Another addition was the reopening about 1882 of a gravel pit at the foot of Middle Incline, to which a siding was laid.

But the enterprise failed; output fell drastically and may indeed have ceased entirely. On Trye's death in 1894, the hill was sold to Mr. Henry Dale and a steady recovery followed, the tramroads finally developing to a greater extent than at any time since the 1830s. Before 1901, the Brownstone Quarry lines were altered to serve its southeastern corner and at the foot of the hill the tracks had been extended to the depot and kilns beyond. In addition, two branches 60 or 70 yards long were laid westwards from the focal point and examination suggests that one of these was formed by merely relaying the initial part of the 1810 route to the Devil's Chimney.

The old gravel pit at Middle Incline was again abandoned by 1897 and in that year Mr Henry Dale incautiously built a stone dwelling (Tramway Cottage) here for his quarry foreman, in a position obstructing the footpath running beside the incline. This and other actions restricting the access to the hill, a right which had been enjoyed by Cheltonians for generations, led to serious public disturbances culminating in the cottage being razed to the ground in the summer of 1902 without a stone left standing. It was rebuilt and narrowly escaped a similar fate a few years later. The ringleaders, popularly known as "The Leckhampton Stalwarts", were imprisoned, but so intense and prolonged was the outcry that they were shortly afterwards released. Dale was morally defeated in a lawsuit and the hill again became one of Cheltenham's most popular recreational areas. The story of these tumults has been told in my *Old Leckhampton*.

During this unhappy period, quarry output had risen considerably and 50 or 60 trams per day were said to be using the inclines.

About 1905 an extension was built to Dead Man's Quarry, just under the brow of the hill near Trye's first excavation. This required 300 yards of line including a new incline, No. 6, and one of the short branches mentioned above was possibly incorporated in the line. It was abandoned in 1920, and about the same year, the second and last of the inclines, No. 7, was constructed slightly south of west from the focal point, with two short spurs beyond.

When the First World War ended, Dale's Leckhampton Quarries Company, formed in 1899, was reorganized and greatly expanded. Advantage was taken of the 1921 Trade Facilities Act to procure an initial loan of £50,000 and a glowing prospectus envisaged an enormous increase in quarry output.

Action followed quickly. A standard gauge railway was built from a junction with the GWR Cheltenham–Banbury line at Charlton Kings, past Southfields Farm to a long electrically powered incline rising to the focal point where four large gasfired lime kilns were erected. The kilns were supplied with limestone by means of a 2 ft gauge tramway. The bottom section was worked by an 0–4–0 Peckett saddletank locomotive acquired from Lightmoor Colliery in the Forest of Dean. The total length of line just exceeded a mile excluding numerous sidings at Southfields Farm.

About 1922, stone sawing machinery which had been housed in corrugated iron sheds facing the depot was moved to Southfields, but the long reign of the hill tramroads did not end until finally supplanted by the new works in September 1924.

It is worth devoting a little more space to the self-acting inclines or "jennies" as they were known locally. Though simple enough to us, these devices were thought wonderful in their day, and rightly so, for the amount of physical labour saved was enormous. In respect of the number, concentration and unusual design of winding machinery, the Leckhampton inclines were unique in South-West England.

Before 1860, no woods and few houses covered the flanks of the hill and an observer could follow the progress of the Brownstone Quarry trams ascending and descending three inclines in succession. A fine sight and sound they must have presented.

The machinery for operating the Devil's Chimney Incline probably set the pattern for Bottom and Middle Inclines; a horizontal winding drum was employed with its axis straddling the tracks, the trams passing beneath. These drums had a manually operated band-brake and each end of the rope was hooked on to a tram, the descending vehicle pulling up the empty one by virtue of its greater weight.

The inclines, other than Nos. 4–7 which were double-tracked over their entire length, were double tracked over the upper half only, the lower half being single. Switch blades were fitted where the tracks converged and were automatically knocked over by the wheels of the descending tram, thus ensuring that it would ascend on the return journey by the same route.

A peculiar mode of working was applied to the two very steep inclines Nos. 4 and 5. The conventional method was discarded in favour of a continuous chain running round a wheel about 6 ft diameter, similar to a colliery pit-head wheel, but having a vertical axis with the trams passing on either side and beneath it. A similar wheel was of course necessary at the foot of the inclines, and both had peripheral notches to accommodate the links of the chain, braking being in the usual manner. The ascending and descending trams were attached to the chain by a shackle.

The continuous chain system was used until 1922 when No. 4 incline closed. The machinery from the top of No. 5 incline was possibly moved to Middle Incline at some time before 1846 when the latter was modified from rope to chain operation. Bottom Incline was also converted to chains, probably at a similar period, but its drum remained horizontal till the end.

A horizontal wheel instead of the more conventional drum was also used on No. 6 and No. 7 inclines and, at the 1927 sale of effects, four of these fetched £1 apiece.

The inclines varied greatly in length, Bottom Incline being longest. Middle Incline was somewhat shorter and had a steeper slope near the top presumably to compensate for the weight of rope or chain when the tram was in the early stages of descent. In later years, if not

Looking along the route of the tramroad towards Cheltenham, at Tramway Crossing in 1964. Subsequent developments have changed the scene completely.

David Bick

Old Tramroad. A cul-de-sac behind Brunswick Square, Gloucester, about 1966. The houses are now demolished.

The tramroad embankment at Wotton Brook, 1966. This is the last substantial earthwork on the route, and houses now occupy the foreground.   *David Bick*

A fine row of blocks with tramplates at the Barge Arm, Gloucester Docks, 1983. *David Bick*

The tramroad entrance to the docks, long since bricked up. Note the old Midland Railway lines in the foreground. 1966. *David Bick*

The end of the line. The tramroad at the quay, looking towards the docks, about 1850. *Gloucester City Libraries*

The Barge Arm in 1968, looking towards the main basin. *David Bick*

originally, the rails on the precipitous Top Incline, No. 4, were laid on longitudinal timbers with cross transoms, reminiscent of GWR broad gauge practice — a technique which was also used for No. 6 incline to Dead Man's Quarry. Most inclines latterly in use had stretches of wrought iron sections replacing the old cast-iron plates.

Operation had hardly begun when a fault manifested itself which was destined never to be entirely cured; a rope broke. A lady riding in a tram had the misfortune to lose her nose in the crash. Her face was saved by the timely presence of Charles Brandon Trye, who quickly replaced the severed appendage with needle and thread. The outcome of this delicate operation was not recorded. In spite of such accidents, the temptation to take advantage of the trams must have been great — a third class ride is better than a first class walk, especially uphill!

Apart from such utilitarian purposes, the novelty was more than enough to attract the young gallants of the day, and these unofficial jaunts sometimes led to hair-raising consequences. The *Cheltenham Chronicle* reported on 6th June 1816:

> Several accidents having occurred on the Tram Road, from the custom of ladies and gentlemen (to avoid the steep part of Leckhampton Hill) riding up in the empty trams, we would caution the public against the pursuance of so dangerous a practice. Several gentlemen, last week took this method of gaining the summit, but when near the top, the rope at the windlass broke, and the tram descended with indescribable velocity; whereby they were considerably bruised—the slightest obstacle in the tract of the vehicle would most certainly have proved imminently dangerous, if not fatal.

There was a very unfortunate accident in November 1827:

> . . . Two boys, one about seven, and the other about ten years old, were at play on the rail road—one of the trains was descending with upwards of a ton of stone, being let down by a windlass, when the rope broke, and the tram came down with the greatest velocity, and killed both the boys on the spot. The father of one of them was working the windlass.

The inquest was held at the "Hamletts", then a public house, but now known as Tower Lodge, on the main road near the tramroad level crossing. The father's name was Harding and a namesake, perhaps a descendant, looked after Middle Incline nearly a century later.

Wilful damage was another problem for the quarry tenant. In May 1812, John Walford & Co. offered five guineas reward for information of the offender or offenders who had "maliciously and feloniously cut the ROPE (there fixed on the engine) through in three different places".

Even after chains had replaced the ropes, the occasional spectacular accident still happened. In 1904, it was said that when breakages occurred on Middle Incline, trams sometimes leapt 10 ft high and cleared 40 ft in free flight — alarming for pedestrians on the lineside footpath.

Much earlier, in 1819, the inclines had developed faults of an apparently serious but unspecified nature. As a result, "it was determined that a survey should be taken by Hamblett and Mr B. Newmarsh (*sic*)—to see whether they could agree on the requisite repairs and the expense thereof". Unfortunately, details are lacking although it is known that the suggested remedies were carried out.

The quarry trams (locally called "drams") had a capacity of 24 or 25 cwt and their design seems to have changed little. Photographs show a robust timber construction with bodies about 5 ft long having slightly tapering sides contained within the wheel track; one end could be removed to assist emptying. Flat trams carried heavy block stone and all had narrow cast iron wheels with 6 spokes and heavy bosses running on fixed axles.

At the height of the quarries' activity, some 40 trams were in use. Regrettably, none seem to have survived the closure in 1927 although one or two smashed-up runaways, abandoned where they lay, are no doubt buried on the hill.

Ironically, Trye's tramroads and the quarry company itself might have endured much longer had the latter been content with the old methods, for technical and financial difficulties soon arose. Moreover, the heavy blasting and smoke created such annoyance that the whole concern was forced into liquidation. The lavish new plant, buildings and railway were auctioned in August 1927 and realized only a tiny fraction of the outlay.

After this interlude, the Cheltenham Borough Council determined to stop any attempts at reopening the quarries and purchased the hill to conserve its amenities for all time. Sadly, it has suffered over the years from a thorough want of management partly to appease certain "nature-lovers", and the hard-fought lower slopes are now an almost impenetrable jungle.

THE TRAMROAD INCLINES: APPROXIMATE DIMENSIONS

Plan Ref.	Name	Length Ft	Rise Ft	Average Gradient	Built	Abandoned
1	Devil's Chimney	320	120	1 in 2.7	c.1795	c.1830
2	Bottom	830	162	1 in 5.1	1810	1924
3	Middle	730	210	1 in 3.5	1810	1924
4	Top	440	210	1 in 2.1	c.1830	1922
5	—	250	—	—	c.1830	c.1850
6	—	330	118	1 in 2.8	c.1905	1920
7	—	240	70	1 in 3.5	1920	1922

Chapter Eight

The Cheltenham & Cotswold Hills Railway

Few lines projected in England have been based on so slender a foundation as the Cheltenham & Cotswold Hills Railway, but although forgotten for well over a century, its importance at the time was considered to be very great. That such a proposal ever existed was first revealed to me many years ago in Gloucester Record Office by a plan for a tramroad nearly 12 miles long from Leckhampton "to or near a certain hill commonly called Fox Hill in the parish of Lower Guiting". Its date was 1811 and the surveyor, Daniel Trinder.

The purpose of such a railway, ending as it appeared nowhere in particular amid very thinly populated uplands, seemed inexplicable. The existence of a large factory for making stone water-pipes at its terminus, discovered a little later, provided the explanation.

The story makes incredible reading. It begins in the first decade of the 19th century when the Stone Pipe Company was created to exploit a patent granted in 1805 to Sir George Wright of Essex for "cutting pillars or tubes out of solid wood or stone". It advertised stone as a durable and hygenic alternative to wooden water-mains, and well known engineers such as James Watt, William Murdoch and John Rennie risked their reputations in the venture. One, and possibly two Boulton & Watt rotative steam engines supplied the power, and contracts were obtained from both London and Manchester. The latter city required no less than 60 miles of pipes ranging from three inches to several feet in bore.

Since efficient transport was essential, the choice of so outlandish a spot seems astonishing, unless the qualities of yellow Guiting stone as occurring at Fox Hill rendered the decision inescapable. Such was the scale and momentum that in 1810, albeit somewhat late in the day, the directors felt justified in promoting a link with the outside world. They did not believe in half-measures, for the Central Junction Canal, as it was called, was to run from the Wilts & Berks Canal at Abingdon via Witney, Burford and Upper Swell to Stratford on Avon. The length amounted to 60 miles not counting a branch from Bourton on the Water to the Stone Pipe works. Charles Hadfield has related how John Rennie supervised the survey of "this unlikely canal", the estimated cost of which was £470,000 or nearly twenty times that of the Gloucester & Cheltenham Tramroad. Meanwhile the pipes had to be hauled by horse and cart to the Severn, most going via Andoversford and down the very steep Dowdeswell Hill, the present easily graded road being some years into the future.

The resulting damage to the turnpikes created a great outcry, at least 30 tons being conveyed daily through the streets of Cheltenham

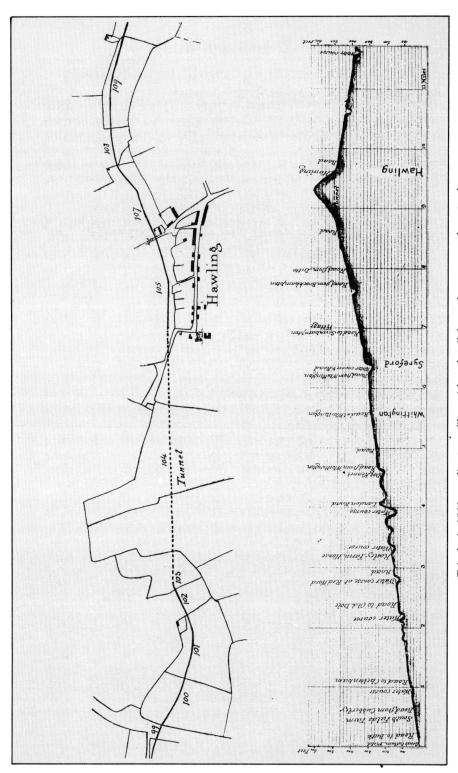

Trinder's 1811 gradient profile, with a detail from the proposed route showing the tunnel at Hawling.

GRO

to the tramroad and thence to Gloucester. We may well wonder how many pipes survived the journey in one piece.

Not surprisingly the canal scheme failed to get its Act, whereupon in the summer of 1811 the Stone Pipe Company, desperate for a solution, launched the idea of the tramroad. It was to form a junction with the Gloucester & Cheltenham line at Leckhampton, and potential benefits to hill farmers did not go unnoticed. To test support the Hon John Dutton (the future Lord Sherborne) and several others inserted a notice in the press for a public meeting as follows:

> . . . to obviate so great a public injury (to the roads) the Cuiting Stone Company have made a proposition to contine the railway from the side of Leckhampton Hill to their Quarry; and have liberally agreed to subscribe a considerable sum, representing at the same time that it would be of great public utility, in as much as the Cotswold Hills would be supplied with coal at a considerably reduced price.

A meeting held at the Frogmill Inn, Andoversford, on 27th August, 1811 discussed the measure, but from a subsequent report it appears the response from landowners was pretty luke-warm.

Nevertheless the Stone Pipe Company had no alternative but to persevere, and announced its intention to apply for Parliamentary powers. The move was generally well supported. Gloucester Corporation concurred, and though there is no direct evidence we can be sure the Gloucester & Cheltenham Railway Company approved. To Cheltonians a relief from heavy traffic would have been a blessing, and one which is still awaited on what is now the A40, 175 years afterwards.

Trinder's profile indicated gradients fairly gradual throughout, climbing continuously to the summit at Hawling with a final descent at about 1 in 90. The reality was worse. From large-scale Ordnance maps we can deduce that the route averaged about 1 in 100 to Whittington, after which it continued more or less on the level to Syreford. Here it crossed the valley and then climbed steeply past Sevenhampton and Brockhampton, through Bakers Wood to the tunnel. From Syreford to the summit it averaged 1 in 60. The final two miles ran downhill at about 1 in 45, twice as steep as Trinder estimated. The gradient in general favoured the stone pipe traffic, but for freight going into the hills it was a different matter.

In such a manner was proposed a railway link of well over 20 miles with the Severn, and one of the longest plateway journeys in the country. Though costly enough the scheme was far cheaper than the Central Junction Canal, and one wonders why it was so long delayed. In the event the Cheltenham & Cotswold Hills Railway nearly got its Act, succumbing only at the Bill's third reading in May 1812.

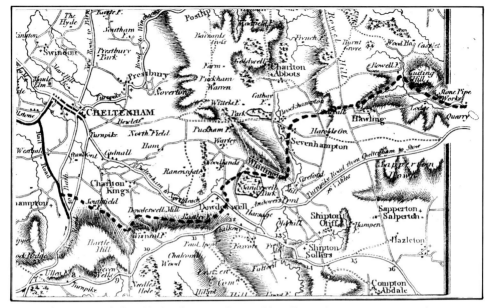

The route of the Cheltenham & Cotswold Hills Railway superimposed on John Cary's map. Note the Stone Pipe works, of sufficient importance to warrant inclusion, extreme right.

The intended route of the line is shown running across the Coln valley north of Syreford, where apparent traces of construction work still survive. Note the much later Cheltenham–Banbury Railway south of the village.

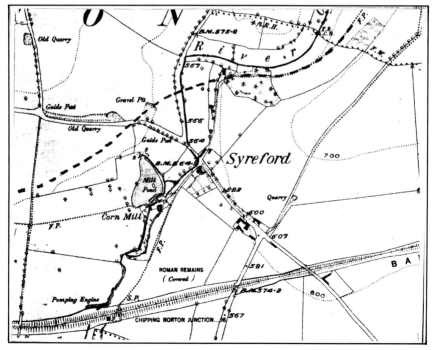

There is a tradition which to some extent physical testimony bears out; that construction actually began in anticipation, an event not without precedent in railway annals. But regrettably this industrial archaeologists' dream could scarcely have come to fruition for the stone pipe bubble was on the verge of bursting.

On testing the complete system in London streets the pipes would literally not hold water, and fractures were so numerous that relaying with cast-iron proved the only solution. The company was wound up and its tools and equipment, though not the engine or boring machines, came under the hammer in 1815.

After having been forgotten for generations the site of the works is now becoming recognised as of national importance, and forms a lasting monument to an extraordinary Georgian enterprise. Since the first edition of this volume much more about the venture has come to light, and its history is being compiled by Dr Hugh Torrens.

As for the Cheltenham & Cotswold Hills Railway, if completed it might well have lasted many years, at least as far as Syreford. The trade in that direction between Cheltenham and towns to the east was substantial, to which could be added building-stone from the Whittington mines, agricultural produce, and coal and general merchandise into the hills.

Whether work upon the line really commenced is an intriguing question to which fieldwork could provide the answer. One suspicious area lies just north of Syreford where the route crossed the River Coln on a high embankment. Beyond, it contoured the steep side of the valley precisely where old maps show a path or cart-track. This is now a broad public path through a wood, and its slight and very uniform gradient (apart from an area of quarry waste) may well have taken advantage of initial earthworks. If the objection be raised, that no railway ever started in the middle, we have only to point to substantial remains near the main road of the abortive East Gloucestershire Railway, begun in 1864 but never finished, only a mile or two to the west.

Those with a fondness for quiet backwaters and bygone times will find few tasks more pleasurable than to investigate whether the Cheltenham & Cotswold Hills Railway did in part, come true.

Chapter Nine
Remnants

The rapid growth of Gloucester and especially Cheltenham during the 50 years of the tramroad's life meant that a great deal of the route became surrounded by shops and houses, the track becoming a thoroughfare for road vehicles as well as tram-wagons. The scene resembled later days of electric trams except that the railway came before the houses, not afterwards. The physical influence of the tramroad on street patterns of Gloucester and particularly Cheltenham is worth recording. The following are a direct consequence.

Gloucester	Cheltenham
Albion Street	Gloucester Road as far as Hayden
Old Tramroad	Queen's Road
Park Road	Andover Road
Millbrook Street (part)	Norwood Street
Armscroft Road (part)	Gt Norwood Street
Elmbridge Road	Leckhampton Road
	Daisybank Road (part)

Because of these developments at both ends and the close proximity of a main road in between, very little of the earthworks or formation of the tramroad long survived closure in 1861. Agriculture reclaimed some of the land, and elsewhere it succumbed to road-widening. Nevertheless, areas of interest still remain.

A convenient point to begin is Gloucester Docks, currently under development as an amenity area. Here the Barge Arm now caters for pleasure boats. It was once full of coal, stone and merchandise barges, and surrounded by sidings from the tramroad. One siding survives as a long row of stone blocks, recently excavated by members of the Gloucestershire Society for Industrial Archaeology. The tramroad left the docks through a gateway in a high wall, now bricked up. This could readily be restored, perhaps with a few yards of track laid down as a monument to the line. Across Southgate Street the route followed Albion Street and curved along the appropriately named Old Tramroad, now a cul-de-sac.

Just inside Park Road the company's depot largely survives, the yard now forming a small private carpark. Beyond Barton Street a footpath takes the route to Millbrook Street. Past Tramway Crossing the line entered a cutting (long since filled in) which was crossed by the sole over-bridge on the whole tramroad. Such was the sanctity of the *Royal William* that the bridge was altered in 1831/2 to give clearance to its funnel.

The Wotton Brook valley was crossed on a substantial embankment near Armscroft Place. This is the last earthwork between Gloucester and Cheltenham and deserves preservation; it is now a path behind some new houses.

The route came into Armscroft Road next to No. 6, and continued along Elmbridge Road on its east side before joining the main road to Cheltenham. The road here made several sharp turns which were by-passed in the 1920s. The tramroad followed these bends though at an easier radius. The ends of the gardens of cottages opposite King Edward VII Inn mark the route.

Some half mile beyond, the line avoided further bends by striking across a field behind the AA office, approaching the road again behind Two Mile Cottage. The next evidence is at Hatherley Brook where Blenheim House stands astride the track.

According to the 1809 Act the brook was to be spanned by one or more arches "not less than 14 yards wide in the clear, such Arch or Arches to be not less than 6 ft high in the Centre, from the surface of the present Ground." The reason for so large a structure is unclear, but at all events it did not materialize, Act or no Act. In January 1818 there appeared an advertisement for contractors to build a new road bridge of three arches "to correspond and adjoin with those under the Rail Road". Interestingly, this still survives as a perfect image of the tramroad bridge which was unfortunately long since demolished.

At Staverton the line took another short cut behind the Plough Inn and across Bamfurlong Lane. Stone blocks have recently come to light at the rear of the Inn car park, and it is hoped to arrange a permanent display.

Beyond the motorway bridge a wide verge marks the route opposite the Staverton Grill, once the Waggoner's Arms. At Arle Court the course is marked by Poplar trees in the centre of a roundabout, and past Benhall the hedge bordering the road is the line's original boundary. At Lansdown Castle a terrace of red-bricked houses occupy the route, and part of an embankment remains beside Lansdown Station. From here to the terminus the tramroad continued to follow the Gloucester Road, the right-hand pavement taking the course for much of the way.

Where the line crossed the River Chelt the original tramroad bridge survives, though somewhat difficult to view. The arch is about 10 ft high, 12 ft wide and 12 ft long; it was greatly widened soon after completion to accommodate the new Gloucester Road, and indeed appears to share the same footings. The southern parapet was apparently taken down soon after 1861 and replaced by a long Cotswold stone wall which still borders the pavement.

At the terminus, a plaque commemorating the tramroad is displayed on the Hop Pole Inn, which occupies part of the site. Across the road the gasworks, which the line served, have been demolished in recent years.

We will now retrace our steps to Lansdown Station where the Leckhampton branch left the main line. Here, a traffic island marks the site of Leckhampton Junction tollhouse, knocked down in 1838. The branch ran up the south side of Queens Road, across Westall Green, along the middle of Andover Road, up Norwood Street and past the Railway Inn (now a shop), the only public house to be named after the line. The area about here has changed little since the last years of the tramroad.

From the Norwood Arms the pavement beside Leckhampton Road occupies the route as far as the Malvern Inn. Still ascending, the line kept to the right of the pavement to the foot of the hill where a factory has taken the site of Trye's tramroad depot. From here, a footpath takes us to the overgrown Bottom Incline, at the top of which are the remains of the old timber-framed winding-drum frame. The path continues on a level to the main road where the lines crossed before entering a shallow cutting and curving beside Tramway Cottage to Middle Incline.

A path runs alongside the incline to the focal point. Straight ahead is No. 4 Incline, now much eroded, rising very steeply to the highest part of the system where in 1972 a fine row of stone blocks was revealed by excavation. They are now largely obscured by vegetation. Beyond, a cutting leads to Brownstone Quarry, which has been converted to arable land.

No. 6 Incline to Dead Man's Quarry is largely submerged in undergrowth. A footpath leading from the focal point along the bottom of the quarries more or less takes the 1810 course to the Devil's Chimney Incline, and stone blocks bear witness to the fact in several places.

Behind the Chimney, grassy gullies reveal the courses of several short tramroad branches to Trye's first quarry. From this spot on a clear day, the eye sees the spreading town of Cheltenham far below, and westwards, Gloucester and the dark hills of Dean where the collieries, apart from a handful of private ventures, are now a thing of the past.

Charles Brandon Trye must often have scanned this scene, waiting for the tramroad to come, and now, nearly two centuries later, it is again time to look to the future. Leckhampton Hill is an important industrial archaeological site and a length of track properly restored with tramplates would make a splendid memorial to Gloucestershire's earliest railway. Compared to £20,000 recently spent on the Devil's Chimney the cost would be little enough. Let us hope it will be done.

Finally we should remember that where the route is now in private ownership, permission to explore should always be obtained.

Appendix I

Tramroad Employees

Apart from those men connected with the Gloucester and Cheltenham Tramroad already mentioned, a few details of others are given below:

Name	Occupation	Known Period
James Button	Weight machine keeper, Gloucester	1814
John Cooke	Linesman	1844
Nathaniel Lambden	Toll Clerk, Gloucester	1824–61
William Wilkins		
Edward Wills	Toll Clerk, Leckhampton	1829–31
Thomas York	Labourer	1839

William Wilkins is buried just inside the churchyard at Westbury on Severn His epitaph reads: "In/Affectionate/Remembrance of/William Wilkins,/Who Departed This Life/July 21st 1867/Aged 81 Years./

He was for Forty three years a faithful/servant of the Gloucester and/ Cheltenham Tram Road Company".

Appendix II

Operating Costs of the Leckhampton Quarry Tramroads

During the nineteenth century, costs of operating the quarries and tramroads changed little and these figures for the early 1880s can be taken as typical.

Apart from gravel, Brownstone Quarry was then providing almost the whole output. Prices per tramload (25 cwt) at the foot of the hill were as follows:

Rockery Stone	3s. 6d.	Rough Wall Stone	3s. 0d.	Rubble	2s. 0d.
Brown Road Stone	2s. 6d.	Coarse Gravel	2s. 6d.		
White Road Stone	2s. 3d.	Limestone	3s. 0d.	Fine Gravel	3s. 0d.

Two small horses and a pair of donkeys were kept for running the trams, usually four or five coupled together, on the level and a woman was given 5s. per week and the tenancy of a cottage at Bottom Incline in payment for hitching the chain to the trams. The quarry tenant paid a royalty of 3d. per tramload and two boys in charge of the animals earned a weekly total of 10s. for their labour.

The expenses per tramload of extracting and conveying the stone could be divided into the following headings:

Average cost of extracting stone … … … … … …	7d.
Running trams from quarry and down Top Incline … … …	1½d.
Descending Middle Incline … … … … … …	1d.
Running trams along level and down Bottom Incline … …	1½d.
Running trams to wharf and unloading … … … …	1½d.

These prices presumably included the empty return journey; thus a round trip involving a distance of 2½ miles and negotiating three inclines each way cost only 5½d. per load (4½d. per ton).

Allowing for all overheads including repairs, total expenditure per annum was estimated at £800. Receipts were £1,100, leaving a clear profit of £300 — an average of 11d. per tramload.

Appendix III

Bibliography

During the past twenty years horse tramroads (plateways) have attracted increasing study including the following publications. The Railway & Canal Historical Society has a Tramroad Group devoted to the subject.

D&C	David & Charles
GSIAJ	Gloucester Society for Industrial Archaeology Journal
IA	Industrial Archaeology
IRR	Industrial Railway Record
R&CHS	Railway & Canal Historical Society

Clinker, C.R.   *The Hay Railway* D&C 1960

Paar, H.W.   *The Severn & Wye Railway** D&C 1963

Paar, H.W.   *The Great Western Railway in Dean** D&C 1965

Jones, Oliver   The Sirhowy Tramroad and its Locomotives. *Presenting Monmouthshire* Autumn 1965

Barter, B.   *Stone Blocks and Iron Rails* D&C 1966

Bick, D.E.   The Cheltenham & Cotswold Hills Railway. *R&CHS Journal* April 1966

Bick, D.E.   Tramplates of the Gloucester & Cheltenham Railway. IA Vol 3, 1966

Bick, D.E.   *The Gloucester & Cheltenham Railway* Oakwood Press 1968

Riden, P.J.   Tramroads in North-East Derbyshire. IA, Nov 1970

Bick, D.E.   *Old Leckhampton* The Pound House 1971

Bean, K.W.   Plate Rails at Godstone, IA May, 1972

Dodsworth, I.C.   Recent Uses of Horse Plateways in W. Yorkshire. IA May 1972

Lewis, M.J.T.   *Steam on the Penydarren* IRR April 1975

Paar, H.W.   The Redbrook Tramroad Incline.* GSIAJ 1977

Reynolds, P.R.   *The Brecon Forest Tramroad.* Swansea 1979

Clissold, G. and Standing, I.   Mr Teague's Railway.* GSIAJ 1980

Rattenbury, G.   *Tramroads of the Brecon and Abergavenny Canal* R&CHS

Statham, I.   The Bullo Pill Tramroad.* GSIAJ 1982

Conway-Jones, Hugh   Excavations of a Tramroad Siding at Gloucester Docks. GSIAJ 1983

Conway-Jones, Hugh   *Gloucester Docks.* Alan Sutton 1984

Weaver, Rodney   *Ancient Britons* (Neath Abbey Tramroad Locos) IRR March 1983

Cook, R.A. and Clinker, C.R.   *Early Railways between Abergavenny and Hereford* R&CHS 1984

* Refers to tramroads in the Forest of Dean

Appendix IV
Sources and Acknowledgements

The Gloucestershire County Record Office has provided much valuable material. Here are the Gloucester and Cheltenham Tramroad Acts, Bye Laws Orders and Regulations, deposited plans, the Sherborne muniments, Trye papers and various documents concerning the Coombe Hill Canal and its projected tramroad. Material relevant to Bristol stone traffic is found under Highway Surveyors and Turnpike headings, and Cheltenham Parish Church records furnish toll permits for the Leckhampton branch. The Griffith & Lewis and Ticehurst, Wyatt solicitors collections are extensive; cursory examination has yielded a few items of interest. (The tramroad company's solicitors in 1861 were Messrs Gwinnett & Ticehurst.) There is also a good collection of plans of the many schemes for rail access to the Gloucester end of the Gloucester & Berkeley Canal.

Sundry matters relating to the tramroad are to be found in the minute books of the Gloucester & Berkeley Canal Company and of the railway companies owning the line after 1836. These are held by the Public Record Office, Kew, where also are share prices for various years and the 1838 Statement of Accounts.

Other information is deposited at the House of Lords Record Office, in minutes of evidence to the Parliamentary Acts directly or indirectly concerning the tramroad.

Development of the tramroad branches and sidings at the docks can be studied by reference to various plans, some of which are stored in the British Waterways Board's offices at Gloucester. A large scale city plan of 1851 is available at the City Museum and the City Libraries have Causton's fine 1843 map, also plans relating to sale of the tramroad ground between Barnwood and Staverton Bridge.

Cheltenham Public Library has numerous townplans showing the tramroad. A large scale plan in the Borough Surveyor's department shows the route, sidings and passing loops in detail.

Local newspapers, principally the *Cheltenham Journal, Cheltenham Chronicle, Cheltenham Examiner* and the *Gloucester Journal,* contain useful material more especially during the tramroad's early years and towards its demise.

Those who have helped in the preparation of this volume are beyond counting, but I would like particularly to thank Isabel Kirby, Humphrey Household, Hugh Conway-Jones, Rev W. Awdry, and the late T.F. Coke.

I am also much indebted to fellow members of the Railway & Canal Historical Society, and to the staffs of Gloucester Record Office and Reference Library who have responded with kindness and forbearance to my endless turning of archival stones in hopes of finding something useful underneath.

Index